MAUD GONNE'S MEN

ANTHONY J JORDAN

WESTPORT BOOKS

Acknowledgements

I would like to thank the many people and institutions that assisted me in this project.the National Library of Ireland, National Archives, the Gilbert Library, Pembroke and Ringsend Public Libraries, the Special Collections at UCD. I want to thank Gerard Whelan of the RDS Library and Ed Mulhall for directing me to sources for the material on James Joyce; Patrick Hugh Lynch for his untiring enthuasism and professionalism, and Sean Kehoe and Kay Gleason colleagues at the James Joyce Museum in Sandycove.I want to thank the members of the Westport Historical Society. I thank the late Anna MacBride White for permission to use her Grandmother's letters and to her late brother Tiernan MacBride who launched my biography on his father.I acknowledge permission, among others, from Aras an Uachtarain & Maxwells to publish the photograph of President Higgins at Fluntern Cemetery in June 2018.
Translations by Penny Russell, Kathryn Burke and Joe McElvaney.

Special thanks to Patrick O'Keeffe for editing the manuscript.

This book is dedicated to

Mary, Antonia, Judith, Fiona, Lily,and Murphy.

&

In Memory of Jarlath Duffy

Past Chair of Westport Historical Society

ISBN 978-0-9576229-4-4

CONTENTS

INTRODUCTION

Maud Gonne's name evokes many different responses from people. There is a mysterious element about her name. Most know that she had a link with WB Yeats and features in his poetry. Others know of an association with Major John MacBride and have an uncomfortable feeling about it, though they are unsure of what that was about. Few know of the French politician, Lucien Millevoye, whom she loved and with whom she had two children. Many know that she was the mother of Sean MacBride, Chief-of-Staff of the IRA, politician and international statesman.

Maud Gonne came largely from a one parent family, whose father Tommy, an English army officer, had a great effect on her persona, despite dying when she and her sister Kathleen were young. Maud and her father were both people of committed action, rather than thinkers. After her father's early death she had to navigate living with older relations until she inherited financial independence and went to live in Paris for thirty years. An essential aspect about understanding her life is that she was a convert twice over, in politics and religion, with all the zealousness that evokes. Her conversion to Irish nationalism became the main focus of her life.

Some problems arise with Maud in that her Memoir, *A Famine Queen*, published in 1938, has been demonstrated to be unfactual in many respects[1]. Another is that she never identified who precisely her daughter, Iseult's father was. Neither did she identify clearly who her half-sister/daughter Eileen Wilson was.

Though she encountered many men in her long life, treating with some in great detail, particularly WB Yeats, whom she saw as a dear friend, but whom she never considered as a marriage partner. He was not a man of action, a Prince, a Joan of Arc, as James Joyce dubbed her in a mocking fashion, but someone who would be useful in helping to free Ireland. Maud changed sides in the Irish Civil War under the influence of her second son,

---

[1] .Mathews Ann, *Renegades Irish Republican Women 1900-1922*, Mercier 2010, p.37.
Ward Margaret *Maud Gonne Ireland's Joan of Arc* Pandora 1990 p. 3.

Sean MacBride, who became the main man in her life. She then avoided meeting the Free Stater Yeats for ten years, throwing in her lot with Sean, the reincarnation of her first baby boy, Georges Gonne-Millevoye. Sean MacBride, the former IRA Chief-of-Staff, who would be accompanied by Maud as he eventually took his seat in an Irish Parliament; Sean MacBride who would play a major role in the Declaration of an Irish Republic; Sean MacBride who, as Minister of External Affairs, would honor his mother, himself and his country in overseeing the postwar repatriation of WB Yeats from France, while rejecting the repatriation of James Joyce from Zurich.

Chapter 1.

THOMAS GONNE

The first man in Maud Gonne's life was her father, Captain Thomas Gonne who was born in London in 1835. The Gonnes were wealthy importers of Portuguese wines. Thomas was not interested in business and he entered the Army by the then-prevalent means of purchasing a commission as a Lieutenant, rather than simply signing up to be a common soldier. In 1855 he purchased the rank of Cornet in the 2nd Regiment of Dragoons. He then transferred to the 17th Lancers based at Cork. In 1857 he went to India to help quell the Indian Mutiny. He learned Hindustani and served as an interpreter, returning to Britain in 1859 to receive the Central Indian Medal. He purchased the rank of Captain in 1862. He met Edith Frith Cook of East Peckham at Colchester where the 17th Lancers were based, and they married in 1865. Their first child Edith Maud Gonne was born in 21 December 1866 at Tongham near Aldershot.

Thomas was posted to the Curragh as Brigade Major of Cavalry in 1868 in the aftermath of the Fenian Rising of 1867. Maud's sister, Kathleen Gonne was born there. The family lived near the Curragh.

Edith Frith Cook, Maud's mother, also came from a wealthy family which manufactured and sold fabrics worldwide. She was to die prematurely in 1871, just five years after her marriage. Her death arose from a difficult childbirth with her newborn third child surviving for two months. The family moved to Howth for a year and latterly Maud and Kathleen went to live with their mother's relations in London for six years, as their father was posted to different locations. These included Vienna, Herzegovenia, Bulgaria, Bosnia, South Africa and India. On 4 March 1879 Col Stanley, Secretary of State for War, referred in the House of Commons that Col Thomas Gonne of the 17th Lancers was incapacitated by an unfortunate accident and unable to accompany his regiment to South Africa[2]. In fact he had been seriously wounded by one of his men while reloading a revolver on St Valentine's Day, an incident which was widely reported in the newspapers in England

---

[2] . *Morning News* 4 March 1878.

and Ireland. Paradoxically this put a hiatus in the peripatetic life of their soldier-father and the two girls got the chance to live with their father for several months while he recuperated. Thomas was then posted to India as commander of the Lancers and the girls went to live in the south of France. They needed a warm climate to strengthen their weak chests. In 1881 Thomas was posted to St. Petersburg and his daughters attended Rosemont School in Torquay. Thomas was re-posted to Dublin as Assistant Adjutant-General at Dublin Castle in 1885. His daughters came to Dublin with him, where Maud enjoyed her position as escort to her father on formal occasions, including Balls at Dublin Castle, where she was introduced to royalty.

Thomas sent his two girls to Paris in the summer of 1886 to their Great-Aunt, on her mother's side of the family, Mary Cook, widow of the Comte de la Sizeranne. Though aged 75 the Comtesse still kept a young English secretary whom she addressed as Figlio and whose secretarial duties were fictional. She had a hobby for cultivating attractive young women and launching them as professional beauties. She was happy to prepare Maud in such a way, perfumed, powdered, hatted and dressed, for display on the Bois de Boulogne. Maud was later taken by her Aunt to Hamburg and shown off at the Casino and put on display in the balconies of theatres. Ann Mathews writes, "Aunt *Mary was determined to find Maud a wealthy man and took Maud on a holiday to Hamburg"* [3] . She became a favoured lady for professional photographers. The Prince of Wales [Bertie] came to Hamburg and Maud was promised an invitation to meet him privately. Maud was in train to be chosen by the Prince as a mistress until her father heard of what was afoot. He came to Hamburg and insisted on bringing her away to see Wagner's *Tristan and Isolde* at Bayreuth. Col Gonne explained to the Contessa about his daughter being invited to meet the Prince of Wales, "*If I refuse to let her go, my military career would suffer, and I don't choose she should be talked about*"[4] . Thus was Maud, as a vulnerable young woman herself, tutored and well equipped to attract suitable men.

Around that same time Thomas got typhoid fever and died on 1 December 1886 at the notoriously decrepit Royal Barracks in Dublin. Maud was 19 and her sister Kathleen 17. This was another devastating blow to the two girls. Maud always remembered two things her father had instilled in her; first, never to be afraid; secondly, that will was a force that could achieve

---

[3] . Mathew's ob. cit. p. 46.
[4] . Gonne Maud, *A Servant of the Queen*, Bookmaster 1983 p35.

anything. His body was returned to England and buried with his wife in Tongham churchyard.

Once again the two sisters went to live in London with their relatives. They spent some time in Ascot with their Uncle Charles who had two young vibrant daughters like themselves, May and Chotie[5]. The Gonne sisters would have preferred to remain at Ascot but the decision was not theirs. Instead they were transferred to live with their legal guardian, Uncle William Gonne in London. He was a very conservative gentleman who tried to instill some rules into Maud's rebellious life. He told her that her father's estate was worthless and she would not inherit any money. Both sisters were presented at the Drawing Room, Buckingham Palace on 2 May 1887 to the Prince and Princess of Wales.

Unknown to his family Thomas had been engaged in a love affair with a lady in Dublin, who had delivered his child that summer of July 1886. Maud encountered the mother of the baby seeking assistance from her Uncle William. As he was dismissing her, the woman turned to Maud, asking for her intervention. It transpired that the woman who was claiming to be the mother of Col. Gonne's baby and was destitute since his death. Maud identified her by the name she had remembered her father asking her to write on an envelope he was posting to a lady. The baby girl was baptized on 10 November in St Mathais Church of Ireland in Dublin. The father was registered as Thomas George Wilson, the name of the clerk on duty[6].

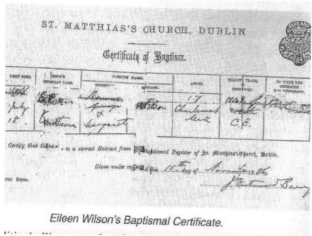

Eileen Wilson's Baptismal Certificate.

---

[5]. Three of these four ladies would make unhappy marriages.
[6]. Gonne Maud, *A Servant of the Queen* [SQ.] Bookmasters 1983 p. 51-55.

The validity of this episode is established when six years later Maud arranged for the mother of her father's baby, named as Mrs Margaret Wilson, to become a governess in St Petersburg[7]&[8]. Eileen initially was left to be looked after by Mary Anne Meredith, the Gonne sister's ex- nanny, who lived in Hampshire.

Uncle William had lied to the Gonne sisters that their father's inheritance had been lost in business transactions and they would have to take on careers. When Maud sought to develop an acting career she developed ill-health. Uncle William then told the truth. He told Maud that aged 21 she and Kathleen would inherit a large legacy making them independently wealthy. Maud then decided to travel again to Paris, to her Aunt Mary, Comtesses de Sizeranne. Uncle William did not demur but sent Kathleen with her as a safety net.

---

[7]. *An Estonian Childhood* by Tania Alexanderi (Jonathan Cape 1987) includes the lengthy story of Margaret Wilson working as a governess in Russia.

[8]. *Deborah McDonald & Jeremy Dronfield, "A Very Dangerous Woman: The Lives, Loves and Lies of Russia's Most Seductive Spy" (2015)[biography of Moura Budberg, nee Zakrevsky, c1892-1974]*

"In 1892 Ignatiy Zakrevsky was visiting England on business. He came into the company of British people.. Among them was Maud Gonne, . She was also the daughter of the late Colonel Thomas Gonne, which made her the half-sister of Margaret's little daughter Eileen, who was now six years old. Maud had been helping Margaret support Eileen since her birth. ....An arrangement was agreed. Zakrevsky would take Margaret with him back to Russia, where she would teach English to his twin daughters, Alla and Assia. Meanwhile, Eileen would be taken care of by Maud. Margaret ended up spending the rest of her long life with the family".

Chapter 2.

MAUD GONNE'S MYSTERIOUS STORY

A STRANGE MEETING

The heat was intense in Central France on that July evening when she first laid eyes on him. Because he made such an immediate impression on her, she believed their souls had met previously. He assured her that was impossible. A storm was raging and Maud was enjoying it as the older Frenchman urged her to come to safety within the hotel with the others. She replied "but how can one leave a storm like this? One must never be afraid of anything, not even death"[9]. Their party was at the Spa town of Royat in the Auvergne Region of France taking the cure. Maud was with Kathleen and their Aunt Mary and a friend named Madame Feline who knew the Frenchman. Maud had strayed to the fringe of the storm and the Frenchman had been asked to escort her back inside.He was immediately taken by her strange retort and putting his arm around her kissed her wet dripping arm, urging her to return inside.

Introductions were made and the Frenchman's name was Lucien Millevoye, a politician and journalist and a supporter of General Boulager, whom Maud had never heard of. Lucien was pleased by this attention because he considered Maud to be the most beautiful woman he had ever laid eyes on. She was very tall with a hauntingly beautiful face and eyes, which though they pierced your soul, did so in a most seductive way. Aunt Mary who was the chaperone suggested that they start a sing song to thwart the storm. The men escorted the women to the music room as the electric storm raged. All the windows were covered and lights turned on, to keep out the sight of the flashes of

---

[9] . S.Q. p. 63.

lightening. Millevoyc's friend played the piano[10]. Lucien presented himself every day at Maud's Hotel for the next week to escort her and the other ladies to the Springs and Promenades. In this way the pair were able to engineer being alone together for long periods. Maud told him she had been ill recently in London after spending sometime acting.

On their next occasion together Maud determined to say as little as possible and let Lucien talk. Lucien was a French Nationalist and a grandson of the poet Millevoye. He was married but was now separated. The passion of his life was the reintegration of the National Territory, the recovery of Alsace and Lorraine.He asked her did she know of its history. She was furious that she did not as he went on to enlighten her. France won Alsace Lorraine in 1648 after the terrible 30 years' war but lost it after the Franco-Prussian war of 1870. It was an insult to the dignity of every Frenchman. "And Frenchwomen too Lucien" Maud added but was ignoredas Lucien continued about Napoleon being a man of genius, a Frenchman, a Bonaparte who made France great. France now wants a master again, who will recapture our provinces. Maud was exhilarated to hear such talk from Millevoye. It brought to mind her childhood days in Howth, when in the cabins of the people she used to see pictures of Irish Patriots - Wolfe Tone, Robert Emmet, Michael Dwyer, Allen, Larkin and O'Brien- hung on the walls beside those of the Sacred Heart and the Blessed Virgin. She realized now that these could be her people fighting to be free. She determined again that she was Irish, not English. She had a mission before her too, if she chooses it. Taking her by the hands Lucien almost shouted, Oh if only you were French, we could fight to recover the lost lands. A man could achieve anything with a woman like you at his side. Will you stand at my side? Maud did not seek to release her hands from Lucien's, but beckoned him to sit in a quiet spot, where they could not be overheard. My country is enslaved by England. She is my enemy. I am Irish, Maud said for the first time ever. England is my enemy too. She defeated Bonaparte. He would have

---

[10] . Lucien Millevoye, born in 1850, was a French journalist and right-wing politician.He was editor of *La Patrie* and a supporter of General Boulanger, whose aim was the restoration of Alsasce-Lorraine to France from Germany. He served as a Deputy in France for many years.

liberated Ireland. Lucien encouraged her saying, you can free Ireland. You can be Joan of Arc. A woman like you can achieve anything if you want to. Maud thought of Tommy who always told her will power was everything. Now like Lucien she wanted to be passionately committed to a cause. I will swear an alignment with you this day Maud, that we will help each other to free our countries. England has always been a natural enemy for France he said. Maud felt physically excited. In the circumstances all she could do was say that she accepted their alignment, until death do us part, or the Freedom of our countries was achieved. She had never more serious in her whole life[11].Maud was to live in Paris for the next thirteen years, as a colleague in Millevoye's work, with regular forays to Ireland to engage in her chosen nationalists events in Ireland.

---

[11]. SQ. pp.64-5.

Chapter 3.

Another Napoleon?

The French have always had a tendency to look for a man of genius who would lead them to greatness. They were willing to trust a charismatic figure and hand over all power to him. General Boulanger [12] was the current *'Saviour'*, a famous and successful man of action who was then setting up a political party and very close to taking power from the politicians, so despised by his followers. Lucien Millevoye and a friend of his Paul Deroulede [13] were disciples of Boulanger. The General was at that time staying with his Mistress Madame de Bonnemain at nearby Clermont-Ferrand. Boulanger wanted to see Lucien and he invited him to a private dinner at a well-known Restaurant *"La Belle Meunire"*. Lucien wished to bring his most recent convert with him to meet his hero who would free Alsace-Lorraine. Maud was thrilled with her invitation to accompany Lucien, but had to deceive Aunt Mary and Kathleen by organizing an excursion for the three of them. At the last moment she feigned tiredness and insisted the pair go without her.

Maud enjoyed meeting such a famous man and was relieved to find Lucien so realistic about his hero. Maud found Boulanger a charming man, assured in female company and completely under the spell of his lady friend. But he didn't strike Maud as a fanatical enough man to carry out his plans regardless. When she asked Lucien for his opinion later, he confirmed her view. Maud enjoyed the secrecy and deception of the evening. Deroulede had succeeded in getting Boulanger offered *a* Royalist Parliamentary Seat in the Charente Constituency. This would have afforded him the opportunity of a glorious entry to Parliament. But Boulanger declined. He wanted Deroulede himself to run in the Election.

---

[12] . General Boulanger was Minister of War, who led a brief but influential authoritarian movement that threatened to topple the Third Republic in the 1880s.

[13] .Paul Deroulede was a French author and politician, one of the founders of the nationalist *League of Patriots*.

Lucien departed for his constituency work the next day, much to the relief of Aunt Mary and Kathleen who were becoming intolerant of Maud's politicization, especially its anti-English element. They tried to argue with her that she was English, just like them, but she was beyond such argument, saying that she was Irish and at last had found her true vocation.

Her first step towards establishing her independence was to travel on her longest journey yet, to visit an old friend in Constantinople, Lilla White, whose father was British Ambassador there. She was to depart from the Port of Marseilles. Aunt Mary did not approve of Maud travelling all that way to Turkey alone, saying that she must take Kathleen with her. Kathleen put paid to that plan by refusing to travel to such a barbarous land, wishing to return to England where she belonged. Aunt Mary finally decided some days later, that as she could not stop Maud they would have to come to Marseilles and see her safely aboard.

Unknown to her companions, Maud had arranged to meet Lucien in Marseilles before departure. They planned to spend some time together alone if possible. He had given her the address of the Hotel where he would stay and could be contacted when she arrived. Maud deceived Aunt Mary as to the date of departure of her ship. She then ensured that Aunt Mary and Kathleen had booked their train tickets back to Paris on the same day she was supposed to sail. She knew that she would be able to convince them to leave her, as it was quite common for travellers to take up board on ship some days before the voyage was to begin. Her plan worked perfectly, and having installed her safely in her cabin and having spoken to the captain, Aunt Mary decided that Kathleen and herself would stick to their schedule.She made Maud promise that she would not leave the ship.

Millevoye and Maud spent the day together in Marseilles. Before he left her back on the ship he bought her a small revolver for safety on her journey

On her return journey from Constantinople, where she had spent a month, Maud's ship docked at Naples. There she received a telegram from Millevoye asking her to come to Paris immediately to the house of Paul Adam, a literary Boulangist figure. He was an associate of Leon Gambetta[14] who played a prominent part in the establishment of the Third Republic. The Boulangists now very much out of favor with the Georges Clemenceau[15] Government which was becoming friendly with England. The Boulangists and the Ligue des Patriotes[16] believed it was in the Republic's interest to forge an agreement with the Czar in Russia. They wanted to send proposals to Russia, but knew the police were watching their movements. Millevoye had suggested that he knew somebody who would be willing to undertake the task and not be suspected by the police. It was to be part of their Alliance.

Maud was introduced to Madame Juliette Adam, who insisted that first the traveller had to be given time to recover from her journey. Only later would she allow the waiting group of men to interview her. She took Maud upstairs and welcomed her as a daughter. She was excited that she was about to get an opportunity to show Millevoye that she was deadly serious in her ambitions of pursuing their alignment.

The operation she was entrusted with was to deliver secret proposals to the Czar's advisor Popodonotzeff. He was head of the Holy Synod in Russia. The matter was extremely urgent and aimed at thwarting British diplomacy on the Continent. Maud offered to leave in the morning. That night she handed her dress over to Madame Juliette who personally sowed the secret documents into the dress. Lucien drove her to the railway station to get a train which would take her as far as Berlin. She thanked Lucien for trusting her with the mission as he responded that together they would go far.

The journey proved tiring though uneventful until she reached the frontier town of Wirballen. There all had to disembark so that their passports could be examined. The Russian Authorities fearful of subversives had insisted on the production of passports for entry. Maud produced her's only to be told to stand aside, as it was defective. Eventually she discovered her passport should have been

---

[14]. Leon Gambetta was a French statesman, prominent during and after the Franco-Prussian War

[15]. Georges Benjamin Clemenceau was a French politician, physician, and journalist who was Prime Minister of France during the First World War. A leader of the Radical Party, he played a central role in the politics of the French Third Republic.

[16]. The League of Patriots was a French far right league, founded in 1882 by the nationalist poet Paul Déroulède.

stamped in Paris, thereby issuing her with a Visa, to enter Russia. She was told it had to be done in Paris and she must return there. Maud was furious. She did not want to fail in her first mission. She also knew it was vital the papers be delivered the next day as the Boulangists knew counter proposals were on their way to the Czar from Berlin, on the Alsace-Lorraine matter [17]. Maud was desperate. She had noticed a Russian man on the train who had tried to catch her eye on several occasions as he passed. She had continued to look out the window to avoid his attention. She had figured him out to be a diplomat as he continually carried a valise with him when he moved. Now she caught sight of him again and decided on a dangerous plan. She asked him to inquire as to what was amiss with her passport. This he did most obligingly. There was a long delay at Wirballen as her new friend tried to assist her.Eventually the message came in on the wire. Permission was granted for her to travel on.

As the train moved slowly out of the station, Igor the diplomat wasted no time in seeking to claim what he thought was his right. Locking the carriage door and closing the corridor blinds, he went on his knees to grasp Maud by the waist and bury his head in her lap. He confessed he wanted to talk to her on the train in Germany but had felt compromised. Maud knew that she had very little time to take control of the situation. She had no intention of giving herself to him and feared she might be forced to display her revolver. But first she would be diplomatic and seek to fool the Russian twice. She explained she wasn't really English but Irish and that in Ireland people despised Englishmen and Frenchmen who were vulgar with women, regarding them as sex objects. But she knew Russian men were more
chiverlous. Her ploy gradually worked as Igor slowed his advances. Maud sought out his hands and taking them in hers, raised him up to sit beside her. Eventually his passion was controlled and he was content to hold hands with his fellow passenger[18].

---

[17]. Alsace-Lorraine was the name given to the 5,067 square miles of territory that was ceded by France to Germany in 1871 after the Franco-German War. It was returned to France in 1919 after World War 1.
[18]. In A Servant of the Queen Maud gives the clear impression that she travelled alone to Russia. In the Adulterous Muse Adrain Frazier writes that "Millevoye came too" further undermining the veracity of Maud's autobiography. p. 60.

The next day Maud completed her mission without mishap. She then called on a Polish Princess named Catherine Radziwill[19], who invited her to stay on for a few weeks. She was shown around Petersburg by a colleague who had worked with her father, Tommy, when he had been British Military Attaché in the city. Maud was appalled by the misery and poverty she saw in the beautiful but cold imperial city.

Among the people she met there was an English Journalist. W.T. Stead[20] of the *Pall Mall Gazette*. Stead was well known as an investigative journalist who exposed many cruel practices around the world, often with sexual connotations. Much of his conversational vocabulary was strewn with references to sexual matters. This aspect of Stead repulsed Maud, all the more so, when he became totally infatuated with her and told her so in written and verbal messages containing lurid language. The main positive thing she saw in Stead was his knowledge of and interest in Ireland. He was in favor of Irish Home Rule and knew many of the Irish Parliamentary Party. Despite her revulsion to his sexual advances, she told him of her desire to help free Ireland from English domination. He told her about Michael Davitt whom he admired greatly being a far finer man than Parnell. He knows the English better having lived and worked in a Mill in Lancashire after his family was evicted from their home in Mayo. He advised her to go to London and see him and to tell him that he sent you[21].

---

[19] . Princess Catherine Radziwill was a notable Polish aristocrat. Born in Russia into the House of Rzewuski, her maternal family was the illustrious Dashkov-Vorontsov. Carefully educated, in 1873 she married the Polish Prince Wilhelm Radziwill.

[20] . William Thomas Stead was an English newspaper editor. He was best known for his 1885 series of articles, written in support of a bill to raise the age of consent from 13 to 16. He died aboard the Titanic.

[21] .SQ pp. 77-84.

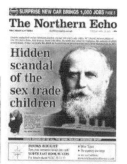

Michael Davitt   St. Stephen's Hall
W.T. Stead.

Maud wasted no time at all in seeking to put her Irish part of
the Alignment into practice. She soon presented herself at the
House of Commons in London and sought an audience with
Michael Davitt. The contrast between those two could scarcely
be more pronounced. He was a man in his early forties whose
whole existence demonstrated the torment of his people. The
son of a small tenant farmer from Mayo whose family was
evicted when he was four years old, Davitt had grown up in
Lancashire. He lost his right arm in a cotton mill accident aged
11. At 19 he joined a secret society known as the Fenians. He
spent 7 years in Dartmoor in terrible conditions. He founded the
Land League in Ireland with Parnell. At the age of 36 he was
first elected an M.P. for County Meath. He had faith in the
decency of the English working class and saw Home Rule for
Ireland as the immediate goal to be aimed at. He was well used
to the duplicity of the English ruling class and it's Government.
Maud on the other hand was from the English Upper class, in
manner and breeding, and with the ambition to become an Irish
Revolutionary.

As Davitt approached the barrier in St. Stephens Great Hall, where
visitors had to wait to meet the members of Parliament, a
policeman announced his name in a loud voice. Maud saw a
tall thin man with a bearded face neatly trimmed. His hair was
receding and his bushy black eyebrows covered intense
brooding eyes. She pushed forward through the waiting crowd
and introduced herself. Davitt couldn't be but taken by her

striking presence and Parisian style. He wondered what business she might want to conduct with him. He ushered her towards a nearby seat and asked her what he could do for her. Davitt was used to dealing with many types of people, but he was immediately suspicious of this eccentric upper class English woman, who seemed to believe Ireland's cause was naturally inimical to England. But being an experienced politician he didn't wish to make any enemies.After a short while he He told her that it was important to preserve the Union of Hearts. He handed her a ticket for the Public Gallery and left. Maud was furious with herself for being so naive, and with Davitt, for being such a Home Rule man and having any faith in England[22].

Maud decided that if she wanted to serve Ireland sho would have to go there and seek out a role herself. She returned to Dublin as an independent woman, who after her earlier times there had a well-established niche in society to return to. All doors would be open to her, should she require it. It was to be the home of one of the wealthiest Unionist families in Dublin, the Jameson's of Donnybrook[23] that Maud first returned to. Ida Jameson's was a great friend of Maud's and both of them believed themselves to be psychic. It was in the garden of 'Airfield' the Jameson home that Maud first declared what her mission in Ireland was to be. *Airfield* was a big rambling house on the South side of the Liffey facing down into Dublin Bay with very attractive curved windows on the North and South wings. The rose garden was to the rear with the vista of the Dublin Mountains as a backdrop.

Ida was the youngest of the Jameson's, all of the family having married and moved out. She too was in love and wanted to marry but her parents objected to her suitor and there was an impasse with them. She was eager and ready to get involved with mischief, particularly with a friend like Maud, whom her parents thought the epitome of female beauty, charm and good sense. That very afternoon Ida returned from the city with a pair of rings for each

---

[22] . SQ. p. 85-87.
[23] . The Jamesons were a wealthy family dealing in whiskey.

of them. The Irish word *'Saoirse'* meaning *'Freedom'* was engraved on each.

The next day Ida took Maud into Trinity College to meet a very good friend of her's Charles Oldham. He was a College lecturer and an ardent Home Ruler even though a Protestant, Ida said adding that he could help Maud with useful contacts. Charles was very amused by Maud's direct approach, but because she was so attractive he took them both to afternoon tea in the College. More importantly though he told them of a club which met monthly-*The Contemporary Club*- to discuss the current political situation. He agreed to take Maud there adding that they never had lady members. He told her that John O'Leary, who would direct and understand her, would be there. Maud asked him to tell her about O'Leary. Charles said he was a Fenian who edited the *Irish People*. He spent eight years in jail and then lived in Paris until he was allowed to return to Irelad. He is also a writer.

The *Contemporary Club* was a gentleman's meeting place. The members were mostly Protestant Home Rulers but also Catholic Nationalists and even Protestant Unionists. It was a cozy chamber with leather chairs and sofas placed around the large room in an informal manner which leant itself to common discussion or a series of semi-private talking groups. Maud, as usual, didn't give any thought to appropriate dress or demeanor. It was just another place, another group of people she was going out to meet. She would take them at face value and know that if the response to her was the same, she would be the center of attraction: not that she sought it or even desired it, but that was the usual way. Oldham led her up the narrow staircase and into the room where about fifteen gentlemen were present. He brought her to the center of the room and above the murmur of conversation he announced *"Maud Gonne wants to meet John O'Leary. I thought you would all like to meet Maud Gonne"*[24]. The response was somewhat muted probably because the members did not like to encourage Oldham's liking for the dramatic and also they had not been consulted about the introduction of this

---

[24] .SQ p. 89.

female. But John O'Leary[25] had been forewarned and knew Maud's presence was to meet him. He immediately came forward with outstretched hands. They were both fine tall figures, immediately attracted to each other for different reasons. *"I am very pleased to meet a leader of revolutionary Ireland. I too want to work for Ireland and I have come to you seeking advice* "she said aloud. O'Leary welcomed her and led herself and Oldham to a sofa.

The debate that evening was about the *Land League*. It was conducted formally enough, with great humor but with force and sincerity. Maud was completely taken aback to find her mentor, O'Leary, castigating agrarian reform and particularly the direct action of the Land League Activists. She did not then understand that he was a land owner himself and unlike her, was not in a position to renege on his own background. She had to refrain from attacking his point of view. O'Leary told her that she must read the hsitory of Ireland and that he would lend her the books.

Maud began to take lessons in practical nursing at the Rotunda, a Protestant maternity establishment. They were short of funds. So Ida Jameson and Maud planned a charity concert in aid of the hospital. It was a fashionable cause organized by well-known ladies and attended by all their Unionist and Protestant acquaintances. But this early stage Maud and Ida were completely into things Irish. They planned a totally Irish evening with songs, drama and poetry. Both ladies performed. The content of the concert would have been mildly surprising to their audience, who might have passed it off as experimental. But when they stood up at the end to sing *"God Save the Queen"*, the music that was played and sung to on stage, and by a small minority of the audience, was *"Let Erin Remember"*: There was consternation in the hall at this obvious insult to the Monarch. During the next week it became a matter of notoriety and a correspondence began in the Letters Page of the Unionist *Irish Times*. Maud was thrilled by it all.

She had made a mark and struck her first blow at England. Unfortunately she entered the correspondence herself and naturally gave her address as *"Airfield House, Donnybrook"*. This proved too

---

[25] . John O'Leary was an Irish separatist and a leading Fenian. He studied both law and medicine but did not take a degree and for his involvement in the Irish Republican Brotherhood in England during the nineteenth century he was imprisoned. O'Leary introduced the poet William Butler Yeats to Irish culture.

much for her hosts, the Jameson's who could not afford to be associated with anti-English sentiments. Within the week Maud had taken up residence in the Gresham Hotel in O'Connell St. Her break with her family tradition was final and public[26].

Maud writes that she received several invitations to perform at this time. Among these she mentions the Celtic Literary Society where she met Arthur Griffith and Willie Rooney. The latter had the embarrassing task of informing her that women were not allowed to become members. Maud retorted that she would have to start a Women's society.

John O'Leary with Major John MacBride

---

[26]. In her account of this concert Maud names Willie Yeats as being one her friends who was present at the charity concert. This is hardly factual. SQ. p. 93.

Chapter 4.

ESTABLISHING HER IRISH CREDENTIALS

The Gresham was one of the most expensive hotels in the city, but Maud was well off and didn't mind everybody knowing that. She entertained there on a wide scale and became well known to the whole spectrum of Irish political and cultural life. But the Gresham had its disadvantages too. It was public and Maud soon felt, correctly, that she was being spied upon by the authorities. She moved out to Nassau St close to the National Library and Trinity College. This too soon became a focal point for people with Irish political and cultural tendencies. Most of her circles were men, who very obviously in the initial stages were physically attracted to her. Hardly any man was impervious to this and many were bold enough to make advances to her. But all were immediately repulsed in a cold and almost unnatural fashion. It became a talking point, all the more so, since she didn't appear to be in the least attracted to any man. She never flirted or engaged in small or romantic talk. Douglas Hyde just then taking his L.L.D. and a noted Gaelic scholar was one of those who frequented her apartment over Morrow's Bookshop in Nassau St.

Despite all her best efforts Maud still had not found what she was looking for. One day she called into the office of the National League opposite the Gresham Hotel. She was informed that there were no lady members but that Tim Harrington would like to meet her the next day. He was about 40 years old and had been a teacher and a newspaper editor. He was secretary of the Land League for the last six years and had been imprisoned twice. His main interest for Maud was that it was he who instigated the *Plan of Campaign* during the Land War which tried to force some leverage from the Landlords to tenants. He was an M.P. for five years and had been called to the Bar the previous year. He was weather beaten in appearance but very able and tough. He had booked a reception room in the hotel and was accompanied by two other Members of Parliament, T.P. Gill and Pat O'Brien. When Maud entered she was surprised and slightly elated to find such a high powered group meeting her. They appeared very cautious telling her that the Government had spies everywhere. She offered her services. Harrington explained that there was a situation in Donegal with evictions being carried out almost unnoticed. He suggested that she might go up there and her presence would attract publicty.

Maud's first cousin, May[27], was just after passing her final nursing examinations in London and three years older than Maud. Maud knew May, like herself, was eager for excitement so she invited her to come with her on a riding trip to Donegal. The ladies duly arrived in the town of Letterkenny where they met the Bishop, Dr. O'Donnell. He was a strikingly handsome man and the youngest bishop in Ireland, who had been educated in the Irish College in Paris and was eager to hear how things were in France from Maud.

The next morning the two ladies set out on horseback for Falcarragh accompanied by Maud's Great Dane, *Dagda*. The dog slowed them down and the weather got wet and windy and cold. At Dunfanaghy they stopped at the local priest's house, unable to proceed further. Fr. Kelly welcomed them and provided rum and hot tea before a roaring fire to try to revive them. He castigated the Irish Parliamentary Party and Home Rule. He believed they had abandoned the people in the fight for land, bringing them so far and when violence broke out, as it had to, abandoning them for constitutional methods.

In that part of Donegal the local landlord was a Colonel Olpherts, who was intent on getting every last penny from his tenants or else driving them off his land. He owned everything from the seaweed on the foreshore to the rocks on top of Muckish Mountain. In Falcarragh Fr. Stephens, took Maud to the local courthouse to see men sentenced for stealing seaweed, others for stealing turf. The penalty was a fine or imprisonment which always meant the latter for these people. Justice was dispensed in

---

[27]. May Gonne-Clay

the court through English, though the accused only knew Irish. A policeman acted as interpreter. Colonel Olpherts had served eviction notices to 150 households and was preparing to carry them out. This meant the literal destruction of their cabins by a force employed by the Colonel. Maud abandoned her tour and returned to Dublin to try and get the National League Members of Parliament to come to the rescue. One of the tactics she put forward was the building of huts to give the evicted somewhere to stay. It was then winter and the people would not survive long in the open. She felt frustrated that her words were not heeded as she planned to travel to London with her cousin May.

MAUD GONNE MEETS WILLIE YEATS

Ellen O'Leary 1831-1889

One of the few women Maud made friends with on the Nationalist side in Dublin was John O'Leary's sister, Ellen. She had been involved with the Fenians, but now was more interested in matters literary. She was a poet and had several of her poems published. Maud encouraged her work. Shortly before returning to London with May, Ellen spoke to Maud about an Irish poet who lived with his family in London, whom she would like Maud to meet. Ellen wrote to the Yeats family telling them of Maud's conversion to the Irish cause. Maud and May got the night boat from Kingstown to Holyhead and arrived into London early the next morning, tired and weary. All the relations were madly keen to hear of their exploits and how Maud was received back into Dublin society.

Maud arranged to call on Mr. Yeats. They had a house in Bedford Park, having left Dublin about eighteen months earlier. Sir Hugh Lane had undertaken to secure commissions for Mr. Yeats, among leading Irish political and literary figures that lived in London. The Yeats, who were living in genteel poverty, much to the dismay of Mrs. Susan Pollexfen-Yeats, welcomed their visitor and were eager to hear the news from Dublin. John Butler Yeats had given up a career at the bar in Dublin to go to London to pursue his aim to become an artist. He attended the Heatherley School of Fine Art. Maud was full of her recent visit to Donegal and said force was the only thing that would free Ireland. She castigated the Home Rule Party as 'time servers' who had no interest with the sufferings of the people. The Yeats family members sitting in their drawing room were shocked by this outburst from their regal looking visitor. However there was one exception among the family as the poet Willie, to the consternation of his father and his sisters, congratulated Maud on her views. His father John Butler, interjected to remind Willie that he was a landlord from which estate they manged to live. His daughters were disgusted by this Parisian dressed female who acted as if they were not in the room. Maud, realizing that she had omitted to do her homework on Mr. Yeats tried to redeem her embarrassment, but was in no way apologetic for what she said. She commented that John O'Leary in whose home she had spent many hours in Dublin,was also a landlord and she counted him among her friends. His sister it was, of course who said I should come to meet the poet in the family. "You mean our Willie and his *Wanderings of Oisin and the Fianna*" Mr. Yeats said, recovering his good humor.

Willie Yeats was completely smitten by this glimmering girl with a pilgrim revolutionary soul, dedicated to Ireland. He immediately felt they were fated to be together and he was prepared to do anything to bring that about. Her body and her openness made him feel passionately desirous of her. For the rest of her brief stay in London, he was her constant companion every evening, much to the annoyance of his poet friend, Katherine Tynan, who castigated

27

Maud for riding unescorted on a sideways carriage. The whole energetic field which surrounded Maud's existence became a magnet for him. He couldn't believe a woman could be so emancipated, so daring, in all she did and said. She told him she was also an actress and was looking for a suitable play which would portray Ireland. He offered to write a play called 'The Countess Kathleen' for her in which a philanthropist sells her soul to the devil to provide for her people in time of famine.

As Willie saw Maud off for to Paris at the boat train at Victoria Station, he laid hands on her for the first time and kissed her on the lips. She did not resist but neither did she respond in any way. She thought of him as a boy whom she could cultivate for the sake of Ireland, a dreamer, a man who woukd be reckoned with in his own sphere. Willie wrote his first poem about Maud after this meeting. He compared her physical beauty to an arrow which had pierced him. Yet he also foresaw difficulties ahead[28].

THE ARROW

I thought of your beauty, and this arrow,
Made out of a wild thought, is in my marrow.
There's no man may look upon her, no man,
As when newly grown to be a woman
Tall and noble but with face and bosom
Delicate in color as apple blossom.
This beauty's kinder, yet for a reason
I could weep that the old is out of season.

---

[28]. Jordan Anthony J. *W.B. Yeats, Vain, Glorious, Lout. A Maker of Modern Ireland*. Westport 2003. p. 99.

Chapter 5.

PARIS AND DONEGAL

Though Maud Gonne devoted herself to Irish revolutionary politics for much of her life, her principal place of residence was in France for over thirty years. There, as Adrian Frazier writes, *"she was part of a political team with him"* [Millevoye] concerned with French revolutionary politics [29]. Lucien was overjoyed to see his Franco-Irlande alignment return to Paris. He met her at the Gare De Nord and brought her directly to his own house on Place Bourbon. She was so proud of her mission and insisted on giving him a lengthy summary of all that she had accomplished. As she told him that she was accepted as a bone fide revolutionary in Ireland he was more interested in quietening her with his kisses. He had news of his own to tell her. His work with the Boulangists was reaching crisis point at that moment. They were in a state of frenzy as they waited for the General to order his followers to storm Parliament. Boulangism promoted an aggressive nationalism which opposed Germany and called for the defeat in the Franco-Prussian War of 1870 to be avenged.

 General Boulanger

[29] .Frazier Adrian, *The Adulterous Muse*, The Lilliput Press 2016, p. 4-5.

General Boulanger had just won an Election in Paris and the Government was expecting the worst. The crowds marched round Place De La Madeleine, down the Rue De Royale and into Place De La Concorde across the river and marshalled outside the Chamber of Deputies. Deroulede and Millevoye wanted Boulanger to give the order. They told him he could be another Napoleon if he was decisive. That night the Government met in disarray awaiting the inevitable they thought, as they huddled fearful, in the Elysee Palace. The President Carnot was prepared to hand over to Boulanger. The General prevaricated, being more interested in attending to the Elysee Palace.sires of his Mistress Marguerite. Most nights Lucien didn't come to Maud at all. Maud did not care, glad that he was involved in his revolution. Some weeks later Lucien returned, distraught. Boulanger was gone to the country with his woman abandoning Paris at the moment could have staged a coup d'etat. Millevoye said that Boulanger prevaricated expecting that he would take power in the next General Election thus throwing the initiative back to the Government.

Lucien was again away a lot as he was to be a candidate in the forthcoming General Election. Their organization, the *Ligue De Patriots,* came under attack from the Minister of the Interior, Ernest Constants. Their leading figures including Deroulede were summoned to court on trumped up charges. The Government's aim was to frighten the Boulangist Camp. The General was easily frightened and fled to Brussels when he heard of a rumour that there was a warrant out for his arrest. Lucien enlisted Maud's assistance in travelling by train to Brussels to persuade Bolanger to return to Paris. They succeeded in bringing the General back to Paris before word of his flight spread. But the Government kept up its war of nerves planning to charge the General with plotting to overthrow the lawful Government of France. It also got a court order abolishing the *Ligue De Patriots.* The Government knew it had no case against Boulanger, but Constants arranged for a colleague of the General's to see a forged warrant for the General's arrest, on his desk in the Ministry of the Interior. The trick worked and again Boulanger fled to Brussels. Milloveye couldn't believe the foolishness of the man. Lucien visited the General in Brussels with Deroulede on a few occasions but came back disheartened. Within a few weeks, the Belgian Government told the General and his lady, they were personae non grata and they fled to England. This did not endear him nor his cause to Maud. He met the Prince of Wales and was guest of Lady Randolph's. He attended the Centenary of the Revolution at a banquet at Alexandra Palace and proposed the Queen's Toast.

Back in Paris Maud and Lucien resolved not to mention the General's name. They had other things on their minds which united them. Maud was pregnant. Maud thought of her father, Tommy, and wished he was alive to hear the news. She remembered him often and felt there was a gap in her life which would be difficult to fill. She knew he would have been proud of her. During those months Paris was the centre of the world's attention with 'Exposition Universelle' drawing 33 million visitors and giving Eiffel's Tower to the city.

The General Election Campaign was a farce from the Boulangist point of view. Their main leadership remained in London; spies were rife in their Paris Headquarters. The second round of voting confirmed the first. In the election of September 1889 the Government won 366 seats, the Rightists 165 and 40 for the Boulangists, including the General, Deroulede and Lucien Millevoye. Boulanger himself was threatened to be disbarred and the defeated candidate declared the winner. Boulangism went into a rapid decline. Maud was elated and so proud of Lucien's election. She told him that she hoped being elected would not change him as it had done to elected members in Ireland, who gladly took their seats in the British Parliament.

Just as Maud was arriving, six months pregnant, in London, Boulanger was taking his leave and fleeing to Jersey, whose climate was recommended for Marguerite. Kathleen Gonne, Maud's younger sister was seriously ill with a liver complaint. Maud did not hesitate on hearing the news and despite her own state, to cross the Channel to help nurse Kathleen. Though they were completely different in temperament, they loved each other loyally. The extended Gonne family felt they too must acquiesce with Maud's outrageous lifestyle and welcome her. Her presence in London though was not announced. Maud was aware that if her liaison with Lucien ever reached the public in Ireland, she would never be permitted to participate in the National struggle. The person she most wanted to avoid was Willie Yeats, who if he heard she was back in London would insist on seeing her. She spent a few most happy weeks with her family helping sweet Kathleen to recover. But Paris beckoned. The new Parliament was due to reconvene in Mid-November. She wanted to be present and had promised Millevoye that she would return to see him take his seat.

As Maud prepared to leave for the station, Willie Yeats arrived on the doorstep. He had heard a rumour that she was in London. Maud did not want to see him in her condition, afraid that he might realise she was pregnant. Kathleen insisted that she see him. Willie entered, hat in hand, very pleased with himself, saying that he had just heard that Maud was in town and apologising for coming unannounced. Maud was very curt, insisting that she must leave immediately. On the way to the station he questioned her about the goings on in Paris and hinted he would like to visit the exhibitions. Maud gave him no encouragement and was relieved when her train puffed slowly out of the station leaving Willie waving goodbye. She felt she had been lucky to escape unnoticed. Willie was full of good manners and too much a gentleman to remonstrate when treated sharply by Maud. But he realized only too well what was happening. Yet because of his passionate love for her, he hoped that in time she might favor him. He wished that he had more material gifts to cherish her with. But alas he had not. Nevertheless he asked her to treat him fairly and gently because his life depended on her. He wrote;

HE WISHES FOR THE CLOTHS OF HEAVEN

Had I the heavens' embroidered cloths,
Inwrought with golden and silver light,
The blue and the dim and the dark cloths
Of night and light and the half-light,
I would spread the cloths under your feet;
But I being poor have only my dreams;
I have spread my dreams under your feet;
Tread softly because you tread on my dreams.

There was a minor demonstration by the Boulangists outside the opening of Parliament. But within, the remnants of the Party were very quiet. It was a glorious day for Lucien, and Maud shared it with him, though discretely, because spies were everywhere and liable to use every situation to the disadvantage of their enemies.

Within two months their baby son Georges was born on 11 January 1890. When she recovered from the birth trauma, Maud was delirious with excitement. She was 23 years old and the mother of a beautiful baby with a man she loved. For a couple of months supreme happiness reigned. Maud had a nurse to help her look after the baby and plenty of household servants at her own house. Lucien was content to pursue his constitutional career for the moment and expected that Maud would remain with the baby in Paris. But she had different ideas and was well used to the idea of babies being looked after by nurses while the parents got on with their lives. She saw no contradiction in this. It led to the first major quarrel with her lover. When he discovered that her intention was to return to Ireland to fulfill her part of their Alignment, he tried to dissuade her. She reminded him that their pact was that he would work to free France and that she would do the same for Ireland. He asked her what she could achieve there. She replied that that was not the point. She reminded him that people were still being evicted in Donegal. She would return there to give whatever help she could. Lucien asked her about her duty towards their baby? She replied that she was not abandoning him that she loved them both but she must go to her other children, saying the nurse would look after Georges.

Maud was soon back in Falcarragh Donegal, where Colonel Orpherts was still evicting tenants. She found that her previous work there had almost made a legend out of her. Stories were told of the two English ladies arriving on horseback to support the tenants. The Plan of Campaign[30] they were involved in was illegal and many people were imprisoned. The regime in prison was so severe as to strike terror into all. Many never survived the experience. Maud mobilized the people, collecting rents due and

---

[30] . This was a stategy in Ireland between 1886 and 1891, co-ordinated by Irish politicians for the benefit of tenant farmers against absente and rack-rent landlords.

bargaining with the landlords on getting reductions. She helped people build mud huts to house the evicted. She travelled incessantly in inhospitable terrain, enduring primitive conditions, putting her own fragile health at risk. She witnessed the forces of Law and Order assisting at the demolition of the people's cabins. She organized resistance to the bailiffs. But a thousand Irishmen, women and children were left homeless in that area during the winter. Their only place of refuge was the workhouse where they died. She felt the old Land League which defended the tenants with force had been taken over by a Parliamentary and Constitutional Movement. This meant that violence was now permissible from one side only- the forces of Law and Order, Maud grew to hate such pacifism.

One day the mail car brought Maud a letter from nearby Dunfanaghy. To her consternation and horror, she found it to be from Milloveve, who had followed her from France. He was in the hotel in Dunfanaghy and ill in bed. He had got the train as far as Derry and ridden from there to Dunfanaghy, but could travel no further. Maud immediately returned with the mail car. Fr. Kelly, the local priest, was with Millevoye when Maud arrived.He was acting as interpreter. Millevoye was in a small bed supported with several pillows. Maud took his hand which was overheated with fever. Maud realized they had to be very discreet as she thanked Fr. Kelly. Millevoye asked her not to chide him for coming. His mission was to bring her back to Paris to look after their son. She saw how sick Lucien was but she rejeced his plan. Within a few days Millevoye began to recover his strength and they began to argue bitterly. At first he spoke of their son in Paris and his future. He felt they both should be looking after him. InParis they could fight on an international stage. He asked her what could she do locally?
Maud knew in her heart that much of what Millevoye said was the truth. But she had to prove herself to those at the center in Ireland, if there was to be a center for her. Now she felt locked into the desperate plight of the tenants and though her health was deteriorating and she was in danger of arrest, she had to go on.

Her motives were not all clear to herself and she didn't wish to begin analyzing herself now. She did what she felt was right and damn the consequences and those who didn't agree. Shortly after this Maud got an urgent request from Tim Harrington M.P.[31] to come to Dublin. It was an invitation to work on a central stage. Maud read the invitation as a final endorsement of her pedigree as a serious and trustworthy opponent of England. But Maud was reluctant to leave Donegal. She was persuaded against her own judgement. There was a Bye Election in Barrow on Furnace in England. One of the candidates came out in favor of Home Rule for Ireland. The Irish Parliamentary Party in Westminster decided to support this candidate, Charles Duncan, a Liberal Gladstonian, and put the Irish question before the English electorate. They wanted Maud to join the campaign. She knew she was being used by those she often despised, but the temptation to experience the campaign was too great. She told Harrington that she would distribute literature and campaign but would not speak. Harrington was a shrewd operator and at the first public meeting in Barrow on Furnace, he engineered to put her on the spot and force her to speak. *"Tell them about the evictions in Donegal"* he shouted from behind to her, as she was led to the front of the platform. Duncan won the Bye Election and the Irish Party felt a great blow had been struck for Home Rule[32].

Tim Harrington. Pat O'Brien MP.

The Government was not amused by Maud's intervention and they decided to move against her for law breaking in the Donegal evictions. She was only back in Donegal a few months when the M.P. Pat O'Brien, arrived in Falcarragh. He had secret information that a warrant for her arrest was to be signed. Maud liked Pat O'Brien and was persuaded that a jail sentence could

---

[31] .Tim Harrington was a journalist, barrister amd nationalist politician. He was an M.P. from 1885-1910. He was Lord Mayor of Dublin three times. He was a friend of John Stanislaus Joyce and wrote a reference for James Joyce as he left Dublin for the continent.

[32] . Ward Margaret, *Maud Gonne* Pandora 1990. p 29.

be a death sentence for her. She agreed to go immediately with O'Brien to get the train for Larne at Stranorlar. He advised her to keep going until she reached Paris as if she was arrested that would depress the people. Maud was sorry to be leaving, but looked forward to seeing Georges and Millevoye again.

Chapter 6.

BABY GEORGES DIES

Samois cemetery. Georges Silvère was interred in the white crypt to the right

In Paris Maud was told by a doctor that her lungs were in such a bad state that she might only have six months to live. Her only chance was to go to live in a warm climate, for several months at least. Millevoye was also ill and he too was advised to go to a warm climate. Together with baby Georges and his nurse, they headed for the South of France and the warm Mediterranean. They settled in a little fishing village called St. Raphael not that far from where Millevoye's parents lived. There they lived an idyllic life, getting plenty of fresh warm air and exercise in the beautiful countryside. Millevoye took up hunting and bought a little rifle for Maud to use. Millevoye was becoming interested in journalism and encouraged Maud to write about her experiences in Ireland. She had an article published in *La Revue Internationale* in Paris which attracted a lot of attention and generated invitations to lecture. Willie Yeats wrote a long article about Maud extolling her work for Ireland and its downtrodden people[33].

---

[33] . *A Servant of the Queen*, Maud Gonne MacBride, Gollancz 1974. pp. 153-5.

Millevoye invited Paul Deroulede to stay with them for a few days. Though Boulangism as a cause was finished, they both still advocated the cause of reclaiming Alsace and Lorraine. Maud was horrified to hear Deroulede say he would be willing to force a Treaty with England, if it would help their cause. Millevoye demurred, conscious of Maud's position and their alignment.

The very next morning a letter arrived from Willie Yeats. Maud was greatly amused to find he had written her Epitaph. Willie knew that Maud's health was not the best. He thought about her working in the wilds of Donegal amid strangers. He imagined that she could have died there. The poor people put her in a very rudimentary coffin. They buried her beneath a cross and sowed trees there. The night sky took no cognizance of her until Willie wrote her Epitaph. _____

A DREAM OF DEATH

I dreamed that one had died in a strange place
Near no accustomed hand;
And they had nailed the boards above her face,
The peasants of that land,
Wondering to lay her in that solitude,
And raised above her mound
A cross they had made out of two bits of wood,
And planted cypress round;
And left her to the indifferent stars above
Until I carved these words:
She was more beautiful than thy first love,
But now lies under boards.

Maud had promised herself that she would regard her cure as complete when she was able to reach the summit of a nearby blue mountain of the Esterol. When this occurred she returned to her Paris apartment and began to give lectures and write more articles on Ireland. Some of the truth of what Millevoye had said in Dunfanaghy occurred to her, she could influence a lot of people from Paris. In Bordeaux she spoke to an audience of 1,200. She found that Catholic Societies were especially interested in hearing her message. She found that reports of her lectures were being carried by the International Press.

When the Conservatives lost the General Election in London, Pat O'Brien wrote to Maud telling her that the warrant for her arrest was withdrawn. She left almost immediately for Dublin. Willie Yeats, who was then in Dublin, went to her apartment in Nassau St, which she continued to retain, to wait to meet her. He had not seen her for quite a long time. He was shocked by her appearance, as she greeted him warmly. She said she was utterly pleased to see him. He was thrilled to hear her honestly spoken words. She had got thin and seemed to have lost the vital forces that emanated from her. Her great beauty had disappeared. Willie was careful enough not to give any hint of his shock. He did not think her vulnerable in any way but her previous aura of invincibility was missing. She was not always looking beyond him, when they spoke. Willie himself was no simple and straightforward love struck man. Though he was born in Sandymount within one mile of where Maud lived as an infant in Donnybrook, he was moved eastwards across the Irish Sea to live in London until he was five. He was not a strong child and didn't enjoy his early schooling. Later in Dublin he avoided seeking entry to University, feeling he would not reach Matriculation standards. He enjoyed country life in Sligo with his cousins the Pollexfens, very much. He wanted to become an artist and attended Art College. He was writing poems and plays from his late teenage years. Like Maud Gonne, John O'Leary and his sister Ellen became his early mentors in Dublin and changed the direction of his life. Through them he decided that the spring from which he would draw his literary themes and inspiration would be Irish, though like Maud, he too would continue to journey and live in and out of Ireland. Unlike Maud he was an intellectual, shy and introspective, always questioning his motives and actions. Unlike her too, he was not wealthy, in fact he was poorly off and had to be particularly careful with his money especially when he was with her. But an interest they had in common was the occult and dreams. Yeats mixed with people in London whose whole lives were directed by their beliefs in extra sensory practices. He was an idealist and believed he had met his soul mate. He waited to be totally united with her. Yet the day after meeting her on her return from Paris, he was independent enough to leave Dublin for the country, to stay with a male friend. Maud had tried in vain to get him to change his plans.

Willie was only gone a few days when he got a letter from Maud telling of a dream she had. They had been brother and sister and were sold as slaves to live unhappily in a distant land. He decided that the time for action was at hand. It was obvious that she felt very close and even dependent on him. He returned to Dublin immediately and called on Maud. They   sat together in her living room, each knowing that a vital moment had come. They were quiet, Willie wearing his horn rimmed glasses with a quif of his hair lying across his forehead, his dreamy eyes determined to cast the dye. Maud was glad he responded to her letter but knowing the price she would have to pay. She wished she could erect signs around the different compartments of her life. They sat a little distance from each other on the sofa not looking at each other. Willie put out a hand and took Maud's hands in his. They were so firm. She dreaded what was happening. Willie said they we were destined to be together and he felt she too realized that. He said he wanted to be her husband and have her with him always. Maud did not react. She did not want to. She wished she could dissolve and Willie with her, into a mystic world where there would be no flesh. She wanted to cry but knew it would be ridiculous. After a few minutes Maud withdrew her hands from Willie's hands.She told him that she was not marriageable, that she wanted to be his friend. Willie did not react to Maud's strange refusal. He was very sensitive to women's moods and felt he could try again later on. He wished to be her friend and be in her company. He wanted to soothe her spirit which didn't appear to know which way it wanted to soar. Over the next few weeks they remained inseparable revisiting places Maud had lived, trying to quench a spirit that was souldering on. He read extracts from 'The Countess Kathleen" which he was writing for her. Suddenly she was gone again back to Paris, summoned, she told him by a Secret Society to which belonged. He also wrote "The White

Birds" commemorating their visit to Howth. He wished that they were both seagulls, which predominate along the cliffs at the hill of Howth. Then life would be simple and straightforward.

THE WHITE BIRDS

I would that we were my beloved, white birds on the foam of the sea!
We tire of the flame of the meteor, before it can fade and flee;
And the flame of the blue star of twilight, hung low on rim of the sky,
Has awaked in our hearts, my beloved, and a sadness that may nor die...

Maud had got a telegram from Millevoye saying their baby son was seriously ill. Georges had meningitis and was dying. He was just eighteen months old with a playful personality all his own. But he was leaving his parents. Maud reacted in a manic fashion, furiously blaming herself and her lifestyle for abandoning her baby. She would not leave the dying baby's side, night or day hoping that her willpower would turn back the illness. Lucien remained with her until the end. Maud became a mad woman losing control of her faculties for a time. She insisted that an elaborate tomb be prepared for the baby's burial. The baby's death certificate dated his death on 31 August but did not carry the names of his parents[34].

In the end she had to be drugged heavily to restrain her. She also felt guilty towards Lucien, that she had let him down and that they must go on together. But Willie remained in her thoughts too and she wrote to him. She told him that a child she had adopted in Paris had died. It was a crazy letter and it upset him to see her suffering so. The following month General Boulanger committed suicide over his mistresses' grave. The next month saw the sudden death of Charles Stewart Parnell, who had been associated with a divorce scandal that divided Ireland. The uncrowned King of Ireland and

---

[34] .Ward Margaret, *Maud Gonne* p. 32.

the leader of the Irish Home Rule Party were both dead.

Charles Stewart Parnell 1946-1891

Maud was soon on the move again returning to Ireland. She carried in her handbag the little knitted booties Georges used to wear. The boat on which she sailed into Kingstown also carried the body of Parnell. Willie Yeats was at the quayside to meet Maud, who was dressed completely in black. At breakfast that morning in a hotel in the city, Maud went through every detail of George's death with Willie. She questioned him about his occult beliefs and said she believed she would meet Georges again. She wanted to become initiated into occult gatherings. Willie was eager to take her along that path. He was frightened by her mental state and he knew she would become dependent on him for initiation practices. Willie noticed Maud attracting a lot of attention in the dining room. Because of her dress and obviously agitated state, people assumed she was in mourning for Parnell and many disapproved and thought it almost theatrical. Maud was oblivious to this. Later in the day she tried to persuade Willie to accompany her to Parnell's funeral to Glasnevin Cemetery. He refused as he hated crowds. Maud was upset, thinking Willie was unusually ill-considerate. She was tired after a sleepless night on the boat, but was determined to go to Glasnevin. It would in some way bring her close to baby Georges.

In the afternoon Maud joined the hundreds of thousands who marched the three miles northwards following Parnell's cortege. It was truly a National occasion, despite his many detractors. As the coffin was being lowered, Maud standing close to the grave saw clearly a shooting star fall from the sky. All those present felt it was a supernatural sign favoring their dead here. Maud took it to also mean that her son Georges was not gone irretrievably from her. She was happy to stand in hallowed ground amid Irish Patriots.

Maud now decided to explore the underworld of Spiritism that Willie was so versed in. Her basic motive was to reestablish contact with her dead infant. They conducted rituals trying to explore their past lives which would explain their personalities. Willie introduced her to George Russell the writer and theosophist who was about their own age. He believed in reincarnation, used drugs, hypnosis and meditation. Willie saw that Maud came to depend more and more on himself. This made him content as he believed he might succeed in his mission to capture her. They travelled to London together so that she could begin a process of initiation to the Order of the Golden Dawn spiritualists[35].

Maud had many psychic experiences herself leading her to believe she had an astral body. Later her old belief in willpower reasserted itself and she didn't complete her initiation, much to Willie's disappointment. Willie pressurized her unsuccessfully, to become his mistress, if she could not marry him. He feared he might lose her unless he could keep her involved with some schemes of which she approved. These would now probably have to be connected with the cause of Irish Nationalism. He realized that she was only going through a phase at the moment and when it and the fear of being arrested had finally passed; she would resume her previous militancy in some shape or other. His *Countess Kathleen* and some poems were published and dedicated to Maud, which included the beautiful lament from the French[36].

WHEN YOU ARE OLD

When you arc old and grey and full of sleep,
And nodding by the fire, take down this book,
And slowly read, and dream of the soft look
Your eyes had once, and of their shadows deep;

---

[35] .This Order involved philosophy, personal development, astrology, tarot divination. Men and women were equal members.
[36] . Yeats WB *Memoirs* p.48

How many loved your moments of glad grace,
And loved your beauty with love false or true,
But one man loved the pilgrim soul in you,
And loved the sorrows of your changing face;

And bending down beside the glowing bars,
Murmur, a little sadly, how love fled
And paced upon the mountains overhead
And hid his face amid a crowd of stars.

Willie confided to Maud that he saw a major role for her in a literary revival, he and others planned to launch. It would be based on all things Irish. A meeting was called for the Rotunda to introduce the aims and objects of the *National Literary Society*[37]. John O'Leary was to be a major force in it. Maud, Willie and John O'Leary were among the speakers.
Maud was to be involved with a scheme to establish Libraries and reading rooms around the country. Willie felt her charisma would be a major attraction in the various towns she would visit. He also realized she would be able to afford the cost involved in so much travelling. The implementation of the scheme proved to be a fiasco with the committee of the Society cancelling it altogether. Willie and Maud fell out over the scheme, each blaming the other for its failure. Willie felt Maud didn't take his aims at all seriously thinking cultural agitation was but a frill. He asked her how could she regard the education of ordinary peope as unimportant? Maud was exasperated in her condescending way. She didn't like to have to explain herself. She didn't want to argue with Willie, but he could be so ridiculous and pompous. Her view was that the people were more interested in where their next meal was going to come from.It is significant that Maud omits all mention of this episode on her autobiography.

Still ill, Maud was brought to France. Willie, totally shattered, headed for Sligo where he might hope to find some peace. Those last few weeks in Dublin were sheer torture for Willie. He was annoyed with himself for having quarreled with Maud. That always

---

[37] .The NLS was founded in Dublin in 1892 by WB Yeats. Douglas Hyde was its first President.

upset him whether he was right or wrong. But then he was not allowed see her even for an instant before she was taken abroad. He knew his enemies conspired in this. They both didn't lack for begrudgers. He also had to endure evil words spoken maliciously about Maud's Parisian existence. In the solitude of the West of Ireland her form never left his mind. He began to continually lust after her. He felt himself almost a wild animal wandering in a desolate landscape seeking and finding inconsolable relief. There he wrote "*Into Twilight*" which lament's his state.

INTO THE TWILIGHT

Out-worn heart, in a time out-worn,
Come clear of the nets of wrong and right;
Laugh, heart, again in the grey twilight,
Sigh, heart, again in the dew of the morn.

Your mother Eire is always young,
Dew ever shining and twilight grey;
Though hope fall from you and love decay,
Burning in fires of a slanderous tongue...

Chapter 7.

ISEULT GONNE-MILLEVOYE IS CONCEIVED

In Paris Maud began to talk about the tenants who had been evicted and jailed in Donegal. Lucien's main concern was for Maud's health and he knew there was no point arguing with her. He said he would organize acountry-wide lecture tour for her where she could collect money for her cause. He suggested they go to Royat again and take the cure there. He would join her in a few weeks.

In Royat Maud's health quickly recovered and she was able to get down to work. She was not an *ex tempore* speaker but always wished to have her speech written out in full. The main theme of her lectures would be the present evictions and the Occupation of Ireland, by England. But she was now in a position to place all of that in a broad historical context, using to the maximum the very close connections with the French Republic. She wrote of the various French expeditions which sailed to Ireland and how so many Irish people had come to live and serve their adopted France. When Lucien came they had an idyllic few weeks together, "*A second honeymoon*" they joked realizing they never really had a first. Maud was so content with Lucien, she was often tempted to analyze why. But fearful of injuring this solid part of her life she didn't, though she knew it was somehow connected with her dear departed and irreplaceable, Tommy who had advised that life is for the living not the contemplation.

The lecture tour was indeed an arduous one covering the whole country from Rouen to Bordeaux to Marseilles, Lyons and many towns in between. Millevoye had played his part, because as well as speaking to full halls, Maud got extensive National Press. During that year a couple of thousand articles appeared in the French Press about Ireland. Maud became most newsworthy. Soon International papers copied and her name spread.

Willie Yeats now trying to earn a living in London was thrilled by her success and wrote to her and told her so. They had no difficulty in making up their quarrel. He felt she had wrested the National Political initiative from the badly split Irish Parliamentary Party and had found her true role as the inspiration of the nation. Willie insured that she got wide coverage in the Nationalist Press in Ireland.

In an interview with Adolphe Brisson in October 1893 Maud admitted that she was enjoying her new found fame in Ireland saying, *"For myself, I am repaid with fame and gratitude for my pains. I embody their hopes. Alas, on my means and on my authority they depend"*[38].

A VISIT TO PORTLAND JAIL

Portland Jail on the Isle of Wight was opened in 1848, where the prisoners were used for hard labor, building the breakwaters of Portland Harbour from nearby quarries. Many prisoners died while quarrying stone.

On a short visit to London to hand over some money for the Donegal prisoners, Yeats introduced Maud to the

---

[38] . Frazier Adrian, *The Adulterous Muse,* The Liliput Press 2016. P. 126.

London Amnesty Association and its Chairman Dr. Mark Ryan, a member of the Irish Republican Brotherhood, a secret society.Dr. Anthony MacBride shared a medical practice with Ryan as well as political views. At Amnesty Maud heard of a recent attempt to force England out of Ireland, that she had been ignorant of, probably because she was a young girl and living on the Continent at the time. From 1880 to 1887 a bombing campaign had been carried out in England with the aim of forcing England to leave Ireland. London, Liverpool and Glasgow came under attack from dynamite bombs. This campaign wan organized and financed by Irish American Fenian groups, led by O'Donovan Rossa and John Devoy. Maud was excited to find that there were people like her, who believed in direct and forceful action. She was also excited to find there was another International dimension to the cause of Ireland. But that campaign had failed and about twenty prisoners were held in jail in atrocious conditions for the past seven years. It was difficult for the Amnesty Association to get accurate information on the health of the men but it was believed that several of them had gone insane. Their cause was a deep embarrassment to the Irish Parliamentary Party which was pursuing a constitutional role.

Three visits annually of twenty minutes duration were allowed to relatives of the prisoners. But as the relatives lived mostly in Ireland or America, many prisoners never received visits. Maud used her family connections to persuade the Home Secretary's Office that as an English lady who had met some of the prisoner's families in Ireland, she might be permitted to visit them and bring news from home. She omitted to tell the Home Secretary that she was Maud Gonne, using her second Christian name, Edith, instead.

Maud travelled to Portland by train. Walking uphill to the prison she saw groups of convicts, chained together breaking stones. Their uniform was a horrible yellow, stamped with black arrows. She had permission to see eight prisoners but on her arrival was told that one of them, an American Dr. Gallagher had misbehaved and was forbidden visitors. This was the man most concern was expressed about, as to his mental health. Maud was shown into a cage with iron bars and told to wait there with the accompanying warder. Opposite her was another cage, just like animals are kept in at the zoo. In between was a passage where a warder sat holding a rifle. In a moment a prisoner was led chained, into the opposite cage accompanied by two warders. The prisoner looked sullenly at Maud dressed in her Parisian finery. She spoke to him, but he was suspicious of her. When he asked about Home Rule, the warders intervened saying no political discussion was allowed. Maud asked how Dr. Gallagher was but again the warders intervened. The prisoner thanked her for coming. Maud wished she could leave, escape. But she had to go through with the whole visit. One prisoner proved unable to speak clearly at all. Another complained about his treatment and was manhandled out of the cage by several warders. The almost ecstasy Maud felt in walking out of that hideous place, made the torture of an afternoon spent in there almost bearable. She had never experienced anything so horrendous in her life. She had never imagined such inhuman and degrading conditions existed. These were Irish Freedom Fighters incarcerated in English prisons. This was another great evil that had to be fought. The conviction of some of the prisoners was in doubt. Maud believed that the English would stoop to any depth when it came to subduing the fight for Irish Freedom. Her visit had a shocking effect on her. For the next few months this is what she engaged in by speaking and publicizing the terrible conditions the men were held in[39].

Maud then returned to Paris and Lucien. She was very much in love with him and happy that their working together was bearing fruit. She was a very well-known personality in Paris holding successful salons to get her message across. Lucien was becoming very successful as a political journalist. His organizing for Maud's lecture tours brought him into contact with many useful people.

She began to speak in other European cities, Amsterdam, Luxembourg. Maud was very much in demand by different groups of Irish people living in Paris. She was invited to their National celebrations especially on St. Patrick's Day. The older emigre families were very well off, but out of sympathy with the values of the French Republic. They were also reluctant to get directly involved with the cause of Irish Freedom, preferring to see it as a romantic dream from their past. On occasions Maud tried to ruffle their somnolence but they were not very responsive. The Irish College students and Irish workers in Paris, she found to be the only people interested among the Irish living in Paris, with current events in Ireland.

Maud tried to interest Millevoye in her spiritualism and occultism. He indulged her but was not a true believer. She spoke a lot to him of reincarnation and how there was a possibility of it occurring within the same family. George's tomb and memorial chapel became a place of frequent visitation by both of them. Maud began to believe that maybe they could seek to reincarnate their dead child, if only they had another. She became convinced of it and tried to persuade Lucien, who was very happy to oblige her, if sexual relations were involved. On one occasion to

---

[39] . SQ. pp. 126-130.

fulfill her fantasy, they made love on top of George's tomb within the Memorial Chapel.

Lucien assured her that she was now doing the real work she was made for, in the Irish cause. He saw her as an International Publicist based in Paris with himself. This is the way he wanted their life together, to go on. There was a possibility that he might become Editor of a Newspaper which would give them both unlimited scope for publicizing their causes. To her great joy, Maud became pregnant again.

Five months later Willie turned up in Paris. He had come over to review the opening night of a new play. To his pleasure it was postponed for two nights and he was able to devote himself to his real reason for coming. He hadn't seen Maud for some time and though they remained in regular correspondence, he wanted to see her. Willie was aware that Maud was different. He found it less easy to communicate deeply with her. She had a new guard around her, which he found difficult to get through. He was still enamored of her, but for the first time, began to feel that she might not become his. The hurt of this was lessened and the realization made possible, by the fact that Willie was no longer a virgin. He had successfully overcome that hurdle and was no longer burdened by sexual frustrations. Neither confided their mutual secrets to each other. Maud accompanied him to the opening night of the play. He noticed that she had difficulty in climbing the stairs, but nothing else.

A few months later in August 1894 Iseult Gonne was born. Maud was blissfully happy. This time she did not hand her baby over to anybody else's care. She told Lucien that she would go nowhere but die with her baby. She decided to move into a new large apartment on Avenue d'Eylau. She had three servants with her. Millevoye had for propriety sake always kept independent quarters, where he conducted his political and journalist work, though they generally saw each other regularly when Maud was in Paris. Maud believed that this new baby had been conceived on George's tomb, and in a real sense, was her baby reborn, though this time as a beautiful girl. Iseult became a real personage to Maud from the first day of her birth. She spoke to her all the time.

Lucien became Editor of his paper - *La Patrie* – and Maud had a readymade vehicle for contributing to the Irish cause without leaving Paris, Iseult or Millevoye. She began to be interviewed personally by visiting journalists as the expert on the Irish situation. All in Ireland were aware of the role she was playing. Those arrested for the Donegal evictions were soon released. Maud was very heartened to hear that Asquith the English Prime Minister had called John Redmond the Irish Party leader, into his office and displayed Press cuttings of Maud's Lectures and Articles. He demanded that Redmond stop this woman and her and her outlandish libels on the good name of England. She was trying to make us out as torturers and criminals, Asquith said. Redmond had to confess that he had no control over Maud's campaign on behalf of the prisoners. Nothing will stop her except the release of the prisoners, Redmond replied.

The English showed little mercy to the dynamite bombers, releasing only three of them due to fears they would die in prison. The Amnesty Association got permission for an American doctor to examine Gallagher. He pronounced him insane. Asquith then had a London Specialist visit Portland Prison and pronounce Gallagher sane. Three years later in 1896, Gallagher was released after spending 13 years in prison. He was insane. Dr Anthony MacBride, a colleague of Dr Mark Ryan and WB Yeats', escorted Gallagher back to America[40].

---

[40] .SQ. p. 194.

In December of that same year of 1896 Willie visited Maud in Paris. One of their nationalistic schemes was to establish a location in Ireland where the Irish leaders in various walks of life could come to renew themselves spiritually. They called it a *Castle for Heroes*. They spent much time together working out elaborate rituals to be performed at their Castle. They experimented with drugs to heighten their spiritual awareness. Though Willie had been involved in a long term physical relationship with an English Actress, he still had not lost all hope of conquering Maud. She of course loved his company and found him stimulating in all things, save sex. He helped her set up a branch of the *Young Ireland Society* in Paris called the Irish Association. He brought a young Irish writer named John Synge to the meeting. But Synge found Maud's Fenianism too vitriolic and left, saying that England could never free Ireland until it felt that an independent Ireland would be a reliable friend. Maud was glad to see the back or the young man, who took Willie's advice and went to live on the Aran Islands and listen to the speech and language of the natives. Millevoye was also a regular attender at these meetings. Willie knew him as an associate of Maud's from her Secret Society work for France. It never crossed his mind that there was anything else between them. Willie found Lucien always very correct.

When Maud decided to launch a new newspaper herself named "L' Irelande Libre- she had enormous assistance from Millevoye. He welcomed the arrival of the paper by writing an editorial about it in his *La Patrie*. He also wrote regular articles for Maud's paper. Many of the Irish community in Paris took it, but its tone offended the old Irish aristocratic element which could have made it a going financial success. Some students and priests from the Irish College assisted Maud, until most were dissuade by their superiors. Many Irish people in Paris wanted Maud to publish their genealogy, wishing to prove their ancient connections. She refused. She also got support from Michael Davitt, Tim Harington and Pat O'Brien though she differed from them politically. She was now quite open about her espousal of physical force as a legitimate weapon to use against the English. She believed Parnell was finished from the day he repudiated acts of violence.

Maud had been absent from Ireland for several years. Though political life was in the doldrums, the cultural renaissance was growing. The National Literary Society which she had helped to found with Willie decided to remove her name from the list of the Vice Presidents. A literary and political Journal produced from Belfast by two women Anna Johnston and Alice Miligan named the *Shan Van Vocht*, objected vociferously, writing that Maud "*Though merely a woman's name, it would have served to connect the Society in the eyes or the Irish race, with what some of us hold to be The National movement*". When Maud read this in Paris she was indignant and thrilled. Once again Ireland was calling her. Iseult was now three years old and a healthy and beautiful girl.

Maud Gonne-MacBride

Iseult Gonne-Millevoye   Lucien Millevoye

EileenWilson-MacBride
Mary Jordan & Tiernan MacBride with Major MacBride's
Boer   War   cane.
.

Chapter 8.

ACTIVISM WITH WB YEATS & JAMES CONNOLLY

When Maud finally returned to Ireland in 1897 there was plenty of excitement in the political air. It was the Jubilee of Queen Victoria's reign and preparations were afoot to celebrate it suitably in Dublin. There were also committees being set up by the Nationalists to celebrate, in the following year, the Centenary of the 1798 Rebellion against the English. They saw this as an ideal vehicle to reclaim the spirit of '98. There was also a third element in the Dublin scene, which Maud found very interesting.

A man named James Connoly born in Edinburgh of Irish parents, had begun agitating for workers' rights, He had been written about in "*The Shan Van Vocht*" and Maud had printed some of his articles in *L'Irlande Libre*. He was the organizer for the Irish Socialist Republican Party. Willie Yeats wanted Maud to meet him and they both went to Connolly's tiny office over a shop in Amien's St. Yeats, who knew everybody on the Nationalist side, introduced a small stocky balding young man to her. Connolly shook her hand firmly and looked her directly in the eye. Maud immediately could see he was a kindred spirit, totally dedicated to a cause. For the next two hours they exchanged views on the current situation. Connolly providing tea for the three of them in cracked mugs. They agreed that there was no point of changing one set of rulers for another, if conditions don't also improve for the working class. They also agreed that Irish Catholic employers were as big an enemy as their English counterparts but that part of the solution was to kick out the English as soon as possible.

This encouraged Maud and she knew she could do business with this man who cared so much about the poor. None of the M.P's she had met had the ideas or vitality of Connolly. Jubilee Day was approaching, The Dublin Convention of the '98 Centenary Committee arranged that they would hold a gathering at City Hall that very night, as a gesture of contempt towards the formal celebrations. As the day approached posters appeared announcing a Socialist Party Public open air meeting for that same afternoon too. Among their speakers was Miss Maud Gonne. She had been consulted by Connolly but was furious as she had understood the meeting was private and wouldn't be publicized. She told Connolly she wouldn't participate. Connolly went to Yeats saying that he would loose all credibility if Maud did not appear as advertised. Willie agreed to speak with her but Maud wouldn't consider changing her mind. In the end he could only extract a promise that she would visit Connolly at home and explain her decision again.

Maud took a carriage from Nassau St. into Sackville St, and down Gardiner St to the tenements where Connolly lived. The smells were the first thing to hit her as she pushed the street door open to reveal a dark and damp interior. Then came the noise and clatter of children on the concrete stairways; she walked up two flights of stairs to number twenty one. In a state of near panic and claustrophobia she knocked on the door. Connolly himself opened it. He was surprised but retained his composure and dignity. He invited her inside to their two room apartment with bare floor boards and sparse furniture; He introduced her to his wife, Lily, who rubbed her hands in her apron before shaking hands with Maud. Several children went very quiet. Maud did not mention the reason for her visit. She felt so honored to be with the Connolly's who were both so witty and lighthearted, despite the deadly seriousness of Jim's work. Before she left they had concocted a few more schemes for the evening of the meeting, which they felt were bound to enliven the proceedings.

The day of the Meeting Willie was among the crowd who listened to Maud speak from the Socialist platform. He was amazed by her public presence and ability to rouse the crowd to anger, one of her lines was, *"How much longer must we endure Jubilee celebrations while there are so many ills to cure in Ireland? Most the graves of our dead go undecorated because Victoria has her Jubilee?"* She told of going along that morning to seek to pay homage to a patriot's grave, only to be turned away. The place was closed down for Jubilee Day[41].

Maud came in for a lot of criticism for her appearance on Connolly's platform. There were always plenty of her ex-friends and new found colleagues who were only too happy for an excuse to blame her. Willie would have none of this begrudgery. He told her not to bother about being criticized by those who regard themselves among the great. He says that future generations would know better.

HE THINKS OF THOSE WHO HAVE SPOKEN EVIL OF HIS BELOVED

Half close your eyelids, loosen your hair,
And dream about the great and their pride;
They have spoken against you everywhere,
But weigh this song with the great and their pride;
I made it out of a mouthful of air,
Their children's children shall say they have lied.

That evening Maud and Willie attended the City Hall meeting of their '98 Committee. The city had been tense all day since Connolly's meeting. The police were out in force expecting trouble. The city was bedecked with flags, Union flags by the unionists and black flags by the nationalists. Just as the crowd was leaving the City Hall they could hear the sound of music. It was a band hired by Connolly coming up Sackville St at the head of a parade of his supporters. In the middle of the parade a group of his supporters carried a

---

[41]. Memoirs 2.112-113.

black coffin with the Queens' name on it. Maud and Connolly planned that their two groups would meet on College Green for an impromptu meeting, but the Police were on the city end of the bridge and when the '98 people arrived, wouldn't let them through. As Connolly and his group approached from the opposite side the police charged them battoning the bandsmen first. The group carrying the coffin rushed to the parapet of the bridge and threw the coffin into the river to the cheers of the '98 crowd who were watching from a safe distance." *to hell with the British Empire*" they cheered. The marchers retreated down Sackville St[42].

Connolly and Maud had arranged for a Magic Lantern [43] display of pictures to be shown on a wall. A huge crowd gathered to watch. Maud brought Willie along to see the display hoping to meet Connolly whose exact whereabouts they did not know. At first it was quite peaceful as pictures of Victoria's reign were flashed up on the wall. A large force of police stood a little way off enjoying the spectacle. Willie was initially surprised at the display as Maud prompted him to bide his time and watch carefully.Shortly different kinds of pictures were displayed showing different aspects of Victoria's reign: the poverty of the tenements, evictions, and jails. The crowd became excited and began to cheer. People began to break away from the crowd and throw stones through any window which displayed Jubilee flags. The police attacked hitting out wildly. Willie and Maud escaped Southside with many others. Some continued stoning windows along the route. At first Willie thought it wrong but soon entered the frenzy of the night and the joyous irresponsibility and sense of power that Maud was experiencing[44].

One woman was batoned to death and Maud and Willie found themselves taking shelter in the National Club. Maud

---

[42] . S.Q. p. 275

[43] . The Magic Lantern used a concave mirror to project and enlarge a slide or photograph onto a wall or screen.

[44] . WB Yeats, Memoirs p. 113

wanted to go out and re-join the crowd but Willie refused to let her. Maud said he made her 'do the only cowardly thing of her life'. Willie and Maud gave different accounts of that night[45].

Later that night they heard that Connolly had been arrested. The next morning Maud presented herself at the Bridewell. She ordered a breakfast from a nearby cafe on the Quays to be sent into Connolly in the cells. She spoke to him briefly telling him she would continue on to speak to his wife about his whereabouts. This done she returned to pay the fine imposed on Connolly in court and have him released. She later wrote him a note of congratulations telling him that his action had saved Dublin from being humiliated by the Jubilee Celebrations.

The 1798 Centenary Committee was anxious to collect funds and highlight their campaign in the U.S.A. But the Committee was split just like the whole Nationalist Movement into the Constitutionalists and the Physical Force element. The Irish Americans were similarly split, each side highly suspicious and antagonistic of the other. After much maneuvering Willie won the Dublin Committee's approval for Maud to travel to the U.S. on a lecture/fundraising mission. The Constitutional element in America regarded her as a spy. John Devoy organised a boycott of her New York meetings. With her pet canary with her as a good luck charm, she spent three months speaking in New York, Boston, New England, Colorado, Denver, Chicago and Ohio. She spoke from the stage to 2,000 people at the Grand Opera House in New York, as the crowd admiring her satin dress and feathered hat. She was joined on tour by James Egan who had just been released from Portland Prison. She had a letter of introduction from John O'Leary to John Devoy but he refused to accept it. Returning to New York she was escorted to her boat by the legendary O'Donovan Rossa, who had been brutally tortured in Dartmouth prison in the 1860s. She had collected £1,000 which was divided between the '98

---

[45]. Ward Margaret ,Maud Gonne p. 49.

Committee and the Amnesty Association. Maud had characteristically come through a difficult mission undeterred by partial hostility and rumor mongering.

Chapter 9.

WILLIE FAILS TO MAKE LOVE TO MAUD

While much of Ireland was concerned with the celebration of the Centenary Year of '98, other parts were experiencing famine. Jim Connolly had just returned from Kerry where the people were starving. He was determined that there would not be a repeat of the passivity that occurred during Black '47. Together he and Maud drafted a leaflet "*The rights of life and of property*". They used liberal Papal quotations to bolster their arguments and get the clergy to support them. Part of it reads "*The very highest authorities on the doctrine of the Church agree that no human law can stand between starving peole and their right to food, including the right to take that food whenever they find it, openly or secretly, with or without the owner's permission*" Maud gave Connolly £25 out of her American money to print the leaflets. Connolly was due to return to Kerry almost immediately.

There was another man who was high in Maud's esteem, editing a newspaper *'The United Irishman'*, named Arthur Griffith. Maud had known him from the period when Douglas Hyde sought to teach her Irish. His wages were 25s weekly. Maud knew he was not married because he couldn't afford to, yet he and his paper were vital to the National Movement. She tried to provide funds to raise his wages to £2-10 shillings weekly. Griffith wouldn't agree. He was a keen admirer of Maud's and like Willie Yeats was poor, but unlike Willie he could never muster up enough courage or passion to proposition Maud. She hoped that she would be able to get Willie to write more Nationalist verse. To this end she introduced him to Griffith who she felt might be able as a fellow intellectual, to inculcate some stronger fervor into his art. Griffith like Willie was no wild revolutionary but a man who was willing to work assiduously with others for a shared ideal. Willie of course knew what Maud had in mind for him and to please her he met Griffith. But nobody was allowed to interfere in Willie's artistic work unless it suited his own purpose. It disappointed him in one way that Maud could still not understand what exactly he was about, in his literary endeavors in Ireland. This upset him but he got used to it. He hoped that his writings would speak sufficiently for themselves. He knew he had to be true to his own muse and not allow himself to become a tool of any propaganda. He was glad that Maud was not successful in diverting him. If she had, he feared that he might have deteriorated as a poet and been content to live an ordinary life. These ideas he committed to verse in his poem of the time called, "Words".

WORDS

I had this thought a while ago,
'My darling cannot understand
What I have done, or what would do
In this blind bitter land.'
And I grew weary of the sun
Until my thoughts cleared up again,
 Remembering that the best I have done
Was done to make it plain;
That every year I have cried, 'At length
 My darling understands it all,
Because I have come into my strength,
 And words obey my call';
That had she done so who can say?
What would have shaken from the sieve?

I might have thrown poor words away
And been content to live.

The French connection was very much to the fore in the centenary celebrations and nowhere more so than in County of Mayo. It was there in1798 the French forces under General Humbert landed and were very successful against the English initially. Enterprising committees were at work in Castlebar and Ballina. Maud was invited to visit and lend her support. There were French graves to visit and " *The Proclamation of the Republic of Connacht* "which was maintained for two months, had to be remembered and honored. At Ballina Maud was told that a famine was then raging in North West Mayo. In nearby Ballycastle people were so weak they were unable to bury their dead. The local doctor was certifying that the people were dying of heart failure, afraid to put starvation down on death certificates for fear of official disapproval. The local Poor House Union didn't have relief to meet the needs. In England Balfour was producing copies of the death certificates denying there was any real hunger?

A properly organised system of relief was required. Heads of households were getting 6d daily for working on the roads. Maud organised meetings, wrote letters, and invited outsiders to visit. The area around Bellmullet was the worst of all. The Congested District Boards [46] and other reliefs came to meet in the local courthouse. Maud drew up a list of five minimum demands and surrounded the courthouse with a few hundred supporters. She threatened the officials that if they didn't agree to meet these demands and release necessary supplies of free seed potatoes, she could not guarantee their safety. She advised them that the forces of Law and Order were several miles away. With the tacit support of the local clergy, she was successful. The people were saved. So Mayo was added to the list of places where the poor revered Miss Gonne, as their savior in time of trouble. No one realized

---

[46] .The Congested District Boards was set up in 1891 to alleviate poverty and congested living conditions in the west and North West. After the Wyndham Land Purchase Act of 1903, it could buy extral land from large estates and give it to small tenants. In 1909 it got compulsory powers.

more than she, how direct action could not be matched by talking in the House of Commons. The *United Irishman* reprted that Maud Gonne *had roused the dormant spirit of a military race, and a wild defiant cheer ran through Mayo towns "*[47].

But the main National meeting was held in Dublin the previous week. It was the culmination of a massive campaign. But Maud was most unhappy with it. She felt it had been taken over by the Constitutionalists and she had not been invited to speak. The biggest single National Event in years had been held in Dublin. Maud attended to hear Willie speak. But she was disgusted and depressed to find herself on the sidelines. An outsider in a movement she had worked so hard to organize.

As ever, Maud then required a period of tranquility and recuperation. Since she had begun to leave Iseult behind her at the Carmelite Convent in Laval where the nuns looked after her daughter, she often returned there. The Chaplain at the convent, Canon Dissard, became a great support to her. Maud explained to him why she could not become a Catholic. She believed in the God of all religions and the Pagan ones as well. But the nuns were praying for Iseult's mother.

Willie soon followed Maud to Paris and they went cycling in the Bois de Boulogne. He could never stay very long because he was usually on some short journalistic assignment which paid his way. Though he never let on to Maud, he had always to be extremely careful with his money, often borrowing when he was going on an excursion with her. She always insisted on paying her own way but Willie wouldn't hear of her paying anything on his behalf. When Willie returned to London he moved into lodgings in Woburn Buildings, Bloomsbury. Maud became a regular visitor for a while. It was a come down from Bedford Park but had its Bohemian aura which appealed to Maud. She usually visited in the late evening. They began to experiment with séances and mediations and ritualistic incantations. He tried to create a Celtic Mythological

---

[47] . Balliet Conrad, 1979 p. 26.

Twilight to enhance their spiritual union. She would often stay until the early hours of the morning. Returning to Dublin they continued the same closeness which became a topic of much gossip. Maud would tease Willie about his reputation, because he had begun to enlarge his social contacts through his literary pursuits, to the Nobility of the Anglo Irish Ascendency.

He had become especially friendly with the Gore-Booths in Sligo and Lady Augusta Gregory of Coole Park. He stayed in both places and was greatly admired and possibly loved by Lady Gregory, with whom he corresponded regularly. She became an Irish Nationalist and was determined to become a force in the development of an Irish Theatrical Tradition. Willie discussed both Maud and Augusta with each other. Maud as usual never thought of the possibilities involved and was astonished to be visited in her Nassau St. apartment one day by Lady Gregory. She was about ten years older than Maud, a little plump and a bit like Queen Victoria, Maud thought. To Maud's further astonishment Lady Gregory inquired about her relationship with Mr. Yeats, asking whether marriage was a probability. Maud was not an especially sensitive or intellectual person but she was hurt by this question. The thought of losing Willie had never occurred to her. He was always there, wherever she was, or else he wrote. She knew she didn't want to loose him, but wouldn't make such an admission to this woman, whom she felt sure, Willie wouldn't want to bed. She replied, much to Lady Gregory's obvious relief that marriage was not on either of their agendas.

Though Willie stayed separately from Maud in Dublin, they usually met early and remained in each other's company for the day. He felt he must consider her reputation. Though Maud wished to be free to pursue her life as she wished, she required a certain amount of moral propriety, to be able to function in a very political society, where women generally had no independent lives, apart from being appendages to their husbands or brothers. But the stress and strain of her double life was beginning to tell on Maud, as she came to depend more and more on Willie. If news of her real French existence became known in Ireland, her public life would come to an end, she knew.

One morning as Willie awoke; he realized he had been dreaming of Maud and for the first time she had kissed him. Rushing to her hotel in Nassau St, he asked her had she dreamt, telling her of what had occurred. She didn't reply. That night after dinner in her apartment, she told him that she did have a similar dream as he. But in her dream they walked hand in hand and were married. Then Maud put her arms on Willie's shoulders, kissed him on the mouth, letting her tongue meet his in a deep passionate moment. He couldn't believe after all these years that the moment had suddenly come when Maud would finally succumb to him. But Willie was not equipped to take the obvious action required. Instead he incredibly abandoned Maud and returned to his hotel.

The next day Maud was full of apologies. Willlie renewed his offer of marriage. She surprised him by admitting a fear of physical and sexual relations. Maud's tone made Willie stop and consider a thought that he had tried to banish from his consciousness over the years. He knew it was not natural for a woman of Maud's beauty to be alone and single. He had feared the worst. Was he now, as he had thought on the brink of success, to be cast down by the revelation that there was indeed another man? Very quietly he asked. She denied it but admitted there had been one she loved earlier. Willie stood up and began to pace the room very slowly, hands behind his back. Maud spoke of selling her soul to the devil as a child and having to put up with her life ever since. Willie asked who was this man? Maud told of Millevoye, of their baby Georges of his death. She told of his reincarnation in Iseult, but that she and Lucien had lived apart mostly since then. She told of Lucien's dependence on her for his work for France, of their Alignment. But she told of Lucien's unworthiness of her too, how he wished her to become a friend's mistress. Finally she told Willie of her life long horror and revulsion of the sex act and that it should only be engaged in for procreation.

How Willie managed to leave Maud's company, he could never quite remember. He found himself across the road in the grounds of Trinity College sitting on a park bench. He was shattered by what he had heard; he was revolted. To think that his Queen could be so mundane as to believe sexual love could only be justified by the issue of children; how barbaric, how pagan, how catholic; he must be the biggest fool in the world. How could he possibly not have discovered or adverted in some small way to the truth; why had he shut his mind to the rumors he had heard about her. Lucien Millevoye and every other person who knew the truth must regard him with contempt.

The next day Willie was full of remorse for his mean and vulgar thoughts of the previous day. He still did not comprehend the totality of what she had told him, but accepted she acted as she had to, being a creature of the Gods. He reverted to his vision of her as his Queen of Ireland, but swore that his carnal pursuit of her must stop. It must be of her volition. He must never force himself upon her. She would be as a sister to him. Theirs's would be a spiritual Marriage. Maud accepted this and left for Paris shortly afterwards to be followed by Willie.

Willie confessed all to Lady Gregory who was in Venice. He wrote, *'I have had rather a depressing time here. During the laslt months, and most of all while I have been here she has told the story of her life, gradually, in more detail, all except a few things which I can see are too painful for her to talk of and about whch I do not ask her'* [48]. Lady Gregory hurried home to comfort Willie. George Russell advised Willie to forget about Maud. But Lady Gregory seeing Willie's torment and knowing he believed he needed Maud to go on, advised him to pursue her in Paris and accept nothing short of marriage. This Willie did. He spent a few excruciating weeks in Paris, hearing in greater detail the crazy story of Maud's life and fatalistic beliefs. Unfortunately for him, he half believed the phantasy, the idealism blinded by Spiritism, the mysticism in which Maud was

---

[48] .Wade 4 Feb 1899, pp 311-312

held. Maud was grateful for Willie's concern for her future but she told him she felt protected for her work in Ireland. She felt that someone was protesting her and despite her outwards activities inwardly she was secure and calm. She declared that as long as she was working for Ireland she was invincible.

Willie didn't know what to reply to such talk, which was shutting him out from any lasting or meaningful involvement. But he did see the parallel between the two of them. She was smitten by Ireland, whatever that meant - and he was smitten by her. Neither of them was going to be fulfilled, he felt, but then neither of them felt they had any choice but to work through their phantasy ordeal. He wrote to Lady Gregory informing her of his despair in Paris. She wrote back advising him to persevere. But she also offered him money to do a European Tour if he so wished. He declined her generous offer saying he could do no more as he was totally exhausted and intended to return home. He began to write this poem at this time which shows his wounded state, being fifty and rejected and dejected.

LINES WRITTEN IN DEJECTION

When have I last looked on?
The round green eyes and the long wavering bodies
Of the dark leopards of the moon?
All the wild witches, those most noble ladies,
For all their broom-sticks and their tears,
Their angry tears are gone.
The holy centaurs of the hills are vanished;
I have nothing but the embittered sun;
Banished heroic mother moon and vanished,
And now that I have come to fifty years
I must endure the timid sun.

Shortly afterwards Willie read that Maud had returned for a visit to Ireland, which showed that she intended carrying on her public role undiminished by personal problems. James Daly, a former prisoner in Portland Jail, had become Mayor of Limerick City. He invited

Tom Clarke, the last of the dynamite bombers to be released, to accept the freedom of the city. Daly also invited Maud to accept the honor on behalf of all her work for the prisoners. Daly had been arrested in Birmingham after an informer betrayed him. He had conducted his own defense saying in the end, "*I love Ireland. I presume you; Gentlemen of the Jury love your country. What is a virtue to you is a crime to me. Be just and fear not. I am no assassin*". Maud was very happy to be associated with these ex-prisoners who had suffered so much for Ireland. Her "*Certificate of Honorary Freedom of the City of Limerick* " read;

"*Be it remembered that at a special meeting of the Municipal Council of the City of Limerick held in the Town Hall in St. on Thursday the 13th of May in the year nineteen hundred with the Mayor in the chamber, it was unanimously agreed that the freedom of the City be conferred on Miss Gonne. And on Thursday the 13th day of December in Council assembled this Certificate was handed to Miss Maud Gonne by the Right Honorable Alderman, John Daly Mayor*"[49].

THE DEAD FENIAN CHIEF

JOHN DALY

---

[49] . Gonne-Yeats Letters p. 136.

Chapter 10

THE IRSH TRANSVAAL SOCIETY

The next opportunity for Irish Nationalists and therefore Maud, to oppose the British Empire lay in the Boer War in South Africa. Her friend Arthur Griffith, who had recently worked in the gold mines in South Africa and returned at the request of his friend Willie Rooney to edit *the United Irishman*, was exploiting the war to whip up anti English feeling. Maud joined in writing articles and speaking publicly on behalf of the Boers. An *Irish Transvaal Committee* was set up at a meeting in the *Celtic Literary Society*, drawing together all strands of nationalism with Maud in the Chair. She proposed a vote of thanks be sent along with a suitable flag, to Major John MacBride who had organised an Irish Brigade out in Africa, to fight the English. This Brigade saw the first action of the war in Natal. MacBride was a very good friend of Griffith's. He was a native of County Mayo and the same age as Maud. He had attended St Malachy's secondary school in Belfast. He was in the Irish Republican Brotherhood in Ireland and the U.S.A. He then emigrated to seek his fortune in South Africa as a tough countryman. The Boers or South Africans of Dutch decent rebelled against the British for a second time. At the start they were fairly successful. But the British responded with massive troop numbers, great brutality, terrorizing the country and establishing concentration camps, until they defeated the Boers[50]. The war was a

---

[50] .

major event for the British Empire and for every other country within it, trying to secede. Opposition to this war united the Irish Parliamentary Party, split since the fall of Parnell. Michael Davitt resigned his seat in the House of Commons." *England's difficulty was Ireland's opportunity*". Maud spoke to a crowd of 20,000 gathered at the Custom House for a protest meeting in Dublin. She and Griffith spoke there and in Cork.

British casualties in the War were high and recruitment became a problem. To assist the cause in Ireland, Trinity College invited Joseph Chamberlain to accept an honorary degree. Maud called a protest meeting of the Transvaal Committee. The Government banned it. The speakers assembled as usual on a horse drawn carriage and proceeded to O'Connell St. for the meeting where a large crowd had gathered. At Abbey St. the police arrested the driver. James Connolly grabbed the reins and drove the horses through the police line, safe briefly amid the crowd. John O'Leary opened the meeting and Maud proposed the motion supporting the Boers. Mounted police arrived. Connolly drove on over O'Connell Bridge, past Trinity, along Dame St. He shouted to Maud *"Will we take the Castle. There are only two sentries there"*. Maud wasn't sure whether he was serious or not, and he continued past pursued by a lone mounted policeman. She regarded Connolly as the bravest man she had ever met[51].

Sean O'Casey witnessed these events and described Maud as ' *A young woman with long lovely yellow hair, smiling happily, like a child out on her first excursion* '[52].

---

[51] . SQ p. 302. Jordan Anthony J. *Boer War to Easter Rising, The Writings of John MacBride*, Westport 2006. pp 1-83

[52] . O'Casey Sean , *Pictures in the Hallway* p.311.

Maud was asked to make another lecture tour to the U.S.A. This time she didn't meet any hostility. She was collecting funds for the Transvaal Committee and *"The United Irishman"*. She stayed in a suite at the Savoy. The Academy of Music was packed to overflowing as she came out on stage. *"Freedom is never won without the shedding of blood"* she said. America continued to sell war materials to the British for the war in Africa. But she collected $1, 000 for the *United Irishman* which helped to keep it afloat[53].

As Irish recruiting numbers to the Army had fallen drastically, the Government decided to send Queen Victoria to rally her Loyal Subjects to the cause. Irish Nationalists were furious. Maud wrote an article entitled *"Famine Queen"*. The issue of the *United Irishman* which carried it was banned. This issue served to bring Maud and Willie together again. Maud knew very well, the enormous damage Willie could do to his literary career by his public declaration of animosity to the Queen's visit as he did when he wrote an article in the Daily Express saying *"Whoever stands by the roadway cheering for Queen Victoria cheers for the Empire, dishonours Ireland, and condones a crime"*[54]. Yeats tried to get Tim Harrington to resign his seat and be replaced by the new Irish Hero of the Boer War, John Mac Bride. Harrington refused. As the day of the visit came, the Government spared no expense titivating the city, enticing people to come out and welcome the Queen. They hired ships to take Belfast workers to Dublin. A party for 5,000 children was held in the Phoenix Park. But in general it was a subdued visit. Many people thronged the route but the Queen was met with a lot of silence as she passed. Both Griffith and Connolly were injured when the police attacked a Transvaal Committee protest. To her utter disgust, Maud was confined to bed in London on that auspicious day in Dublin. But the banning of the *United Irishman* only served to give her offending article world coverage.

---

[53] . *Irish World* 10 February 1900.
[54] . *Daily Express* 3 April 1900.

When Maud arrived in Dublin a few days later, she was astounded to find Griffith in jail for defending her honor by horse whipping a journalist who had printed an article claiming Maud was a British spy. She took a Libel action against the journalist and won[55].

The following issue of Griffith's paper made the suggestion that Dublin children who had foregone the Party put on for the Queen's visit should be recompensed. Maud discovered many women who had tried but failed to be given roles in the various National Organizations. They soon got together themselves with Maud as President and formed "*The Patriotic Children's Treat Committee*". Thirty thousand school children got a marvelous party in the Phoenix Park, magnificently organised by the women. Afterwards they decided to stay together and formed "*The National Woman Committee*". This soon was formally established as - *Daughters of Erin* with Maud as President. They were a mixture of ages and backgrounds; some related to well-known figures but others independent women. Their aims were to establish the complete independence of Ireland and to combat English influence on the lives of the people. They fostered Irish culture. Maud got Willie Yeats, Padraic Colum and George Russell to write for their artistic performances. They ran classes for children. For the first time in her public life, Maud was to experience the companionship of women working with her in the National struggle. They choose St. Brighid as their Patroness. They operated out of an upstairs room in Great Strand St and soon their pupils began to figure as prize winners in the Feiseanna. Maud would later claim in her Memoir, *A Servant of the Queen* to be the main motivator behind these activities though this work has been dubbed as *"...a masterpiece of self-aggrandizement, a fantasy, a masterpiece of self-absorption"*[56].

True to Maud's principles, the *Daughters* started a direct action campaign to thwart army recruitment. The army changed their rules making it obligatory for the soldiers to sleep in Barracks. So at night Dublin was full of Redcoats with their girlfriends. The *Daughters*

[55] . Jordan Anthony J. *Arthur Griffith with James Joyce & WB Yeats – Liberating Ireland*, Westport p. 44.
[56] . Mathews Ann. *Renegades*, Mericer Press 2010, p. 37.

brought out leaflets saying Irish girls were disgracing themselves by consorting with the enemies of Ireland. They distributed these in Sackville St. Regular fist fights developed between the men folk of the two sets of women. A Limerick Augustinian priest wrote leaflets saying anyone taking part in an unjust war was guilty of mortal sin. The police were reluctant to prosecute anyone as they were afraid that the huge numbers of illegitimate babies in the workhouses could be highlighted. The Augustinian priest told Maud he expected she would become a Catholic and he was praying to that effect.

Now that Maud had become a member of a group and saw how effective women united were, she and others wanted closer association and recognition by other organizations. The secret I.R.B. had drawn its members from all sides. But now, there was a feeling that it was necessary to draw all groups together openly in a Federation. This was done in Cuman Na nGaedhal a separitist movement, advocating withdrawal of the Irish Members of Parliament from London to Dublin. The Celtic Literary Society, Daughters of Erin, '98 Centenary Clubs, Athletic Clubs, Hurling Clubs, Young Ireland Societies, Literary Clubs all joined. Willie Rooney presided at its first Convention. John O'Leary became President. Irishwomen had finally been accepted as constituent members of the National Movement. This had never been a priority of any kind with Maud, but she now realized that women could be very effective and valued their friendship and company.

The Dublin Transvaal Committee was invited to Paris by the Paris Municipal Council and welcomed at the very impressive Hotel de Ville. Maud and Arthur Griffith were among the delegation. On July 13th they were all entertained by their hosts at a Banquet on Ave. Clicy in Montmartre. Because of his impecunious state, Griffith stayed with Maud in her apartment. This pleased him greatly. The city was en fete for Bastille Day. The whole group was invited to a performance of 'The Valkyrie' at the Opera. Milloveye joined them. During the interval Maud was surprised to hear him criticize the leading Soprano and nominate another singer as just as good. Later that evening a female friend of Maud's, Madame Avril, indicated that said lady had become Millievye's latest protégé. Maud understood what she was being told about Lucien and was not very surprised. Later when Maud read the latest issue of Lucien's '*La Patria*' and was angered to find an article under his name saying Germany was now the only enemy of France. She reread it carefully and realized it was not written by him at all. She knew his style too well. But he was the Editor. Personal betrayals she was prepared to forgive and overlook, but the betrayal of their Alignment, the dropping of England as the common enemy, never. Now the truth began to dawn on her. Lucien was never serious about her cause. While it suited France to be Anti English, that was fine. But Clemenceau and his pro English party were successful in their seduction of Anti English sentiment. Maud made enquiries and discovered that the article was in fact written by the soprano Lucien had spoken so highly about at the Opera. She decided to part with him. Their Alignment was finished. Iseult was all that connected them and she knew Lucien was her father.

Before Griffith and Maud left for Dublin they received unexpected, but welcome, news that Major John McBride was on his way from South Africa to Paris. He would be arrested if he returned to England or Ireland as a treason felon. They set out for Gare de Lyon to greet him. Griffith was his old friend so that they had no problem identifying him. He was a wiry red haired deeply tanned man. They all returned to Maud's apartment and spent the whole night in conversation. Maud was enthralled to meet a real hero who had fought against the English and was now ready to go into Guerilla Warfare against them in Ireland. He thanked Maud for her support and told her stories about the Flag she sent out to *The Irish Brigade*, how it inspired his men. Maud had never spent such an exhilarating night in her life[57]. She was so proud of MacBride, so proud to have been of assistance to him. The disappointment caused by Milloveye was being quickly forgotten. MacBride was the same age as she and unmarried.

---

[57] . Gonne Maud MacBride, *A Servant of the Queen*, Gollancz 1974. P.319

Maud's Apartment site on Avenue d'Eylau

The *Paris Young Ireland Society* held a reception for McBride which Maud attended with Griffith. The latter could see that Maud was attracted to his friend, something he had never noticed before.

Griffith knew that there was a lady in Ireland who was very fond of MacBride and looked forward to his return. She had sent two loving letters to him to South Africa on the battlefield, praying for his safe return. She made constant requests to Griffith and John's brother, Joseph MacBride, for any news of him. Her name was Anna Johnston, poetess, who together with Alice Milligan ran the *Shan Van Vocht* in Belfast. She was a most beautiful and sincere woman[58]. These are some extracts from her letters:

Lisnaveane

Antrim Road

Belfast

Feb 21 1900.
Dear Major MacBride,

---

[58] . Jordan Anthony J., *Boer War to Easter Rising, the Writings of Major John MacBride*, Westport Books 2006. P.167. Anna wrote under the name of '*Ethna Carbery*'. She married the writer Seumas MacManus [1867-1960] on 22 August 1901 and died prematurely on 2 April 1902, aged 37.

...I wrote you some time ago and would have written again, but that I fear you may be beyond the reach of correspondence. Occasionally I hear of you from the Editor of the United Irishman and your brother, and every scrap of news is welcomed, I need hardly say. We were greatly grieved that you were wounded at the Tugela, but sincerely hope that you are quite strong now. We watch the success of the fight with intense interest and pray for the success of our friends with all our hearts.
Beannacht leat a Sheaghain and keep the Green Flag and the Vierlieur flying.
Success and glorious victory; and that our own dear land may soon be a free nation!

With kindest regards from every one of us
Always your <u>friend</u>
Anna Johnston

I meant this letter to be a letter of introduction but I must send you shamrock: it would never do to miss it. We pray for you every day
My mother, father and sister send you regards[59]

Another letter dated <u>April 10 1900 read</u>;

Dear John,
        This is to introduce Mr. Charles Mallon and friends from Belfast. I hope they may prove useful to you.
...Your brother Joe most kindly let me have a peep at your last letter home and I was much gladder than I can say, to know that you were so well after all the fighting. We are absorbed in the war here and my "Sister of Charity" prays for you every day. The Queen's visit has upset all the snobs in the country. They are like mad people now with loyalty. Miss Gonne has been ill in Paris or I do believe she would have headed an insurrection here...
Well John, you lost Cronje and we feel greatly for the loss...when shall we see you again and shake hands once more? I wonder. But believe this, that your friends in Lisnaveane send you warmest

---

[59] . When I first located these letters in the NLI, in 2005, there was also a separate neatly folded page within the envelope which to my astonishment contained the remains of the shamrock, after 105 years! MacBride had retained the letters up to his execution.

*regards and heartiest wishes for your success and safety and hope
you will live, as you say, " to lead a charge in old Ireland".*

*With my sincerest friendship
Your friend
Eithne ni Sheagson*

However in Paris the firm advice to MacBride was that it would be suicidal for him to return home. He should go on a Lecture Tour of the U.S.A. where he would be welcomed. MacBride said that he was not a public speaker but Maud said that she would write them for him. They spent several days together as Maud compiled a bulky set of fiery speeches for delivery in the U.S.A[60].

Major MacBride stayed at the Vanderbilt Hotel in New York City. He gave interviews to the world's press, talking about ' *the empire of hell'.* He proved quite successful there but was personally miserable. He had been used to the rough life of the outdoor guerilla and found the people and the hotels overpowering. He also missed Maud Gonne. He wrote to her saying that unless she joined him, he wouldn't continue the tour. Maud answered his call. Together they attended one last function in New York City. About two million native born Irish people lived in the United States of America. Most of them had gone there out of absolute economic necessity. A large proportion of them had come from the western seaboard of Ireland, where life was harsh. The County of Mayo was one of the foremost places the emigrants left. John MacBride had been one of these a few short years previously. The emigrants maintained close ties with their native places and were very proud of where they came from. The Mayo Women living in New York organised a dinner in honor of MacBride, a native of Mayo, and presented him with an Illuminated Address, which showed how close they were with events in Ireland. Part of it read;

> *"Address to John MacBride, Major and Organizer of the Transvaal Brigade   In recognition of your sterling work and unimpeachable patriotism, we beg to make this trifling overture; for women though we be, we have always had a kindred regard*

---

[60] . Manuscript 29,820 NLI

*,an unbounded love for the brave soldier' of our race who lives
and fights for the cause of liberty. We cannot restrain from
placing on record the intensity of your patriotism,
the intensity of your patriotism , the unselfishness of your
character , and the splendor of your manhood   We are fully
aware of the meagre amount of good done by constitutional
nationalism. This is why we greet you as a true representative of
the warlike Gaelic race unconquered still through centuries of
Saxon oppression. We are also aware that you were nominated
by your friends and admirers in your native county to a seat in
the British Parliament. Notwithstanding that the purpose of such
a nomination was solely to emphasize the feelings of the people
against the barbarity of England's war on the Boers, a certain
faction in Ireland for its own base purposes and to the eternal
chagrin of all true nationalists, brought about your defeat.We
know of course that you would never stoop to take an Oath of
Allegiance to the enemies of your country. The reign of physical
force seems to be once more resurgent to the truth that by force
of arms alone can Ireland ever hope to gain her longed for
independence.*

MacBride and Maud Gonne then ventured together out into the
great continent. She did the secretarial and publicity work.
MacBride did the talking. They formed a good team, drawing
crowds of Irish and Irish Americans to hear their message and
contribute dollars to the cause. They had a very difficult meeting
with John Devoy who was the acknowledged political leader of
the Irish in the U.S.A. He had been a Fenian and served time in
jail to be released on condition that he emigrates. He came to
dominate *Clan na Gael* the main Irish American organization,
which though riven by factional splits was still to play an
important role in helping various Irish nationalist leaders who
came to America looking for help. Devoy did not approve of
Maud at all. She and MacBride were preaching revolution against
England to people who had become constitutionalists in their
adopted country. Maud knew he was speaking the truth and was
glad his view of affairs married with her own.

After a few weeks Maud realized that MacBride could well complete the tour without her. He had become an accomplished performer, even if he did still read much of his speech. But the main reason she began to think of returning home was that she knew MacBride had fallen in love with her. Her old magic affected him too and he proposed to her in St. Louis. Donal McCracken writes of this episode from *A Servant of the Queen*, "*She later claimed that it was on this coast to coast tour that John MacBride proposed to her. If that is so, MacBride was flattered and dragooned into it*". John wrote to his mother in Westport, telling her what a wonderful woman Maud was[61]. Maud refused his offer, saying that while Ireland was at war, she would not marry. He did not accept that at all, saying, Ireland will be at war for the foreseeable future.

Shortly after this a *Deus ex Machina* appeared in the shape of a telegram to Maud from Arthur Griffith in Dublin. His friend and mentor Willie Rooney had died and he was distraught. He begged Maud to return to Dublin as soon as possible. Griffith was MacBride's friend too so he felt he couldn't object. Maud used it as an opportunity to get away from MacBride, but it was not to Dublin she returned for quite some time.

[61]. McCracken Donal *MacBride's Brigade* Fourcourts Press 1999 p.150

Chapter 11.

MARRIAGE AND RECONCILIATION

When Maud arrived in Paris from the U.S.A. she received an invitation to London for her first cousin May's wedding. Her sister Kathleen wanted her to stay with her family. Willie Yeats had also written to inquire how her American tour had been. She wrote to him inviting him to see her in London at Kathleen's house. Maud's arrival at Kathleen's house always created tremendous excitement. Maud was so exotic herself and usually travelled with several pets, either dogs or birds or monkeys. This time she had smuggled a tiny alligator from America for Kathleen's boy who was seven. All the children were ecstatic, jumping around in their pyjamas. Maud thought the domesticity very boring.

After dinner Yeats arrived to see Maud. She was still in her dark travelling clothes and black veil she then wore, instead of a hat. Willie complemented Kathleen on how well she looked. She told him that it was hard work for a woman to retain her beauty. He agreed but added tha an effirt must be made, being critical of Maud's casualness with her appearance. He thought she looked unhappy and worn out. At 35 her natural beauty needed more conservation if she was to stand out in a crowd. The contrast between the two sisters that evening made such an impact on him that he turned it into a poem. Willie recalls being alone with Kathleen and Maud. They spoke of poetry. Willie tells the Ladies how poetry must appear obvious and almost spontaneous, not showing any of the difficulties of composition. Unless the poet can work so, it would be as well to undertake servile manual work. The world does not understand that the poet's work is more difficult than manual work and the poet is held up to ridicule. He wrote:

ADAM'S CURSE

We sat together at one summer's end,
That beautiful mild woman, your close friend,
And you and I, and talked of poetry.
I said, 'a line will take us hour's maybe;
Yet if it does not seem a moment's thought,
Our stitching and unstitching has been naught...

The next day they made their customary excursion to Westminster Abbey to see the stone- *Lia Fail*- which had been stolen from Tara where the High Kings of Ireland were sworn in.

Willie's lodgings at Woburn Buildings had become a meeting place of the famous literary people; John Masefield, Robert Bridges, Mrs. Patrick Campbell, Bernard Shaw, Annie Horniman who was trying to rival Lady Gregory as his Patron. They all recognized Maud as his inspiration. In a conversation with Maud he asked her was she happy. Her response said that she did not think of happiness, that she was busy with an exciting life. He told her that he still wanted to marry her. Maud responded that she would not make him happy. She told him that he was happy. He wrote beautifu poetry about her and that marriage would be a cruel come down from that. Domesticity was soul destroying she assured him[62].

They discussed the possibility of stealing the Great Stone and transporting it back to Ireland. Then they went back to Willie's rooms. Maud admired how he had made them so comfortable with so little money. She sat in his new leather armchair, until he told her it was his latest present from Lady Gregory.

---

[62] .Yeats Gonne MacBride Triangle p.28-29

Willie had recently finished his Play - *Cathleen Ni Houlihan*-written for Maud and dedicated to Willie Rooney. It was to be performed under the auspices of *the Irish National Theatre Company*. Maud was delighted with it and agreed to play the lead, only then finally returning to Dublin after Griffith's urgent summons. It was a one act play set in rural Ireland in 1798. An old woman visits a tiny Irish house. She is the personification of Ireland who in the end reveals herself as a young girl with the walk of a Queen. It was a highly charged patriotic, a theatrical and Nationalistic masterpiece. Yeats became President of the Irish National Theatre with Maud, Lady Gregory, Doughlas Hyde and George Russell as Directors.

Maud returned to Paris where she began to seriously consider John McBride's proposal of marriage. There were many points in its favor both personal and political. The latter was the easier to sort out. McBride was a folk hero in Ireland already and must have a political future there. As such Maud could become aligned to him and continue her own work. She would be able to introduce Iseult into such a family under some guise or other.

John McBride had secured employment in Paris as secretary to the correspondent of the American *Sun* and *Laffan's Bureau* at two pounds a week, but remained very poor. Maud had to be very circumspect with him as far as money was concerned and social niceties. He believed the man should always be able to pay for his lady. When Maud once suggested taking tea in his small apartment, he thought such a suggestion most improper and almost indecent. Yet he relented and they spent many hours in his tiny attic discussing how they might free Ireland[63].

Kathleen heard a rumor of Maud's friendship with MacBride. She wrote to Maud asking her to be very cautious and suggesting that even at this late stage, she accept Mr. Yeats's proposal. Maud in one of the rare occasions she opened up her true self to anyone, admitted that she always preferred to be envied rather than pitied.

---

[63] . SQ p. 155-156.

She said she was getting old. She still considered marriage an intolerable burden, but circumstances forced her to consider it. She felt a marriage to MacBride would be natural.

John MacBride's mother advised her son against marrying Maud. She said they came from two different worlds. His brother Joseph also told him that Maud could not make him a good wife. She was too independent, he said. Arthur Griffith, who knew them both very well, told Maud that she was the only female friend in his life. He also knew her singlemindedness in pursuit of her aim. He said that she and MacBride were as different as chalk and cheese. For Ireland's sake; he implored them not to marry. "*Forgive me, but while there is still time, think* "he wrote. She dreamt that her father Tommy also advised against the marriage[64].

The most upsetting scene Maud had to experience occurred when she went to the convent in Laval to tell Iseult of her marriage. On hearing her mother's message, Iseult cried and said she hated MacBride[65]. Iseult still had regular contact with her father and feared MacBride would supplant Millevoye in the wider family circle. Canon Dissard was delighted to hear of the marriage plans. He was also glad, as were the nuns in the convent, to hear that Maud had decided to go all the way and be received into the Catholic Church. They had prayed long for that to happen.

John and Maud showed their various letters to each other, letters of congratulation as well as letters of dire warning. They were both silent for a long time after reading them until Maud stood up and laughed aloud saying ," *John, those whom the Gods love die young a short life and a merry one , let us go to dinner*"[66]. That night she dreamt of her beloved Tommy, who implored her not to marry. But the dye was cast. Not even her Father's words could stop her.

The *United Irishman* newspaper had carried a notice announcing, "*A forthcoming event which has occasioned great interest and pleasure among Irish nationalists. Miss Gonne, who some time ago*

---

[64] .SQ p. 349
[65] . S Q. 348
[66] . Gonne MacBride Maud, A Servant of the Queen p. 349.

became a Catholic, will be formally received into the Catholic Church on Tuesday, at the Chapel Des Dames de St Therese, Laval, and her marriage will take place before the end of the month"[67].

During the lead up to the wedding Maud often thought of Willie. She knew she owed him an explanation - a hundred thousand explanations - but what could she say to such a man? How could she explain herself? She was afraid to contact him, only sending him a telegram at the last moment. He was just about to deliver a lecture in Trinity College Dublin when he received it. He read the message and continued to finish his lecture. He had no memory afterwards of what he had said or how escaped from the College. The scale of the betrayal numbed him and he went into shock as he walked the streets of Dublin in a haze. When he came too, much later, recuperating with Lady Gregory at Coole Park, his bitterness was profound. He wrote two poems baring his soul. He saw his own mistakes for having prolonged his love for Maud past the time it could flourish. Though they were so close in many ways, yet she changed suddenly, and he became an outsider. He sees that women need to be kept on a string where love is concerned. Otherwise they will take it for granted and the lover becomes a plaything, to be discarded, as he was.

OH NOT LOVE TOO LONG

Sweetheart, do not love too long:
I loved long and long,
And grew to be out of fashion
Like an old song.

All through the years of our youth
Neither could have known
Their own thought from the other's
We were so much at one.

But O, in a minute she changed-

---

[67] . United Irishman February 14 1903

87

O do not love too long,
Or you will grow out of fashion
Like an old song.

NEVER GIVE ALL THE HEART

Never give all the heart, for love
Will hardly seem worth thinking of
To passionate women if it seem
Certain and they never dream
That it fades out from kiss to kiss;
For everything that's lovely is
But a brief, dreamy, kind of delight.
O never gives the heart outright,
For them, for all smooth lips can say,
Have given their hearts up to play.
And who could play it well enough
If deaf and dumb and blind with love?
He that made this knows all the cost,
For he gave all his heart and lost.

The wedding itself took place at the Church of St. Honore d'Eylau in Paris. The priest officiating was Fr. Van Hecke, Chaplain to the Irish Brigade in the Transvaal.The flags of the Irish Brigade and The Daughters of Erin were carried at the low key ceremony. The civil proceedings took place at the English Consulate where they were received very coldly. MacBride had fears he might be kidnapped there. At the reception Maud proposed the final toast, *"To the independence of Ireland* ".He was thirty six, she thirty five[68].

The couple went to Algeciras in Spain on honeymoon from which Maud writes mysteriously,*'from which we both thought there was a great chance we would never return'*[69]. Maud said in later years that they were part of a Clann na Gael plot to assassinate Edward

[68] . *Yeats-Gonne-MacBride Triangle* p.38.
[69] . *SQ* . p. 350.

VII in Gibraltar but that MacBride returned to their hotel drunk that night, refusing to say what had happened. The next day they both returned to Paris[70]. Margaret Ward writes that the Kings visit occurred two months later in April and speculates that Maud's insertion in her autobiography *"sounds like adventurous fiction"*[71].Ward, like Nancy Cardozo, makes no mention of drunkenness, rather she says Maud's main complaint was of the cold. It would appear that whatever occurred the honeymoon was a disaster.

About two months after the marriage, George Russell wrote to Willie Yeats, telling how a friend of his, who did not know Maud personally, dreamt of her. In the dream she came to the dreamer crying, saying that she did not know what to do or where to hide. A month later Maud came to London.Willie was given the news of her whereabouts as he was in London too. He was very nervous. One part of him wanted to stay away from her, to avoid more hurt. He had scarcely recovered from the earlier trauma he had suffered. But the news that all was not well in the marriage affected him. He could not be sensible where she was concerned. She was his Queen, no matter what. He felt he must go to her. He must do whatever he could for her. Maud never doubted for a moment that he would come. Thoughts flitted through her mind that maybe, she would respect him more if he ignored her presence.Willie called to see her at Kathleen's house. He saw Kathleen first and asked if it was true Maud's marriage was in trouble. Kathleen confirmed that indeed it was so, adding that she should have married him.

Maud had made a terrible mistake. She married in a sudden impulse of anger, she told Willie, and seeking to conform, she had lost her independence. Willie forgave her, writing to Lady Gregory of his friend's anguish. There was no question but Willie was more than willing to be reconciled with Maud and he wished his public to know that. Willie's betrayal by Maud was not a private matter. It was of immense public interest. Everyone knew she was his muse and that

---

[70] . *Gonne Yeats Letters* p 168.
[71] . Ward Margaret *Maud Gonne* Pandoro 1990 p . 78.

her marriage was bound to affect him deeply. Some condemned Maud because they feared her action would dry up his output of love poetry. He compared her action to one who cannot see or hear reason, but who acted in fury. His public feared for him. But now all is well, she has returned and he is happy as in the past. But he begs her to stay close as their separation tormented him.

RECONCILIATION

Some may have blamed you that you took away
Tice verses that could move them on the day
When, the ears being deafened, the sight of the eyes
Blind With lightning, you went from me, and I could find
Nothing to make a song about but kings,
Helmets, and swords, and half-forgotten things
That was like memories of you—but now
We'll out, for the world lives as long ago;
And while we're in our laughing, weeping fit,
Hurl helmets, crowns, and swords into the pit
But dear, cling close to me; since you were gone,
My barren thoughts have chilled me to the bone.

There is little doubt that from the start both Maud and John realized that they had made a terrible mistake. He, an independent-minded and proud man had married into an all female household which saw him as a usurper, an oddity, one who did not belong in their world. He was dependent on his wife for bed and board and even for pocket money. Maud saw this immediately and allocated a large sum of money to him from which he would have a steady income. She wrote, "*About two months after our marriage I gave John a present of 100 pounds, which was what I spent on myself for dress and journeys, outside housekeeping expenses. I wanted him to have the same, as I felt it was humiliating for a man to have to come and ask his wife for money, whenever he wanted anything. I also thought the capital would be the means of helping him to get some position. I know work is difficult to get in Paris"*[72].

Maud went to Dublin mainly to escape her husband, but also despite her personal tribulation, to help organize opposition to the impending visit of the new King, Edward VII. Tim Harrington was now Lord Mayor of Dublin and Griffith's paper, *The United Irishman*, reported that Dublin Corporation was about to give an official welcome to his Majesty. It had been three years since his mother's visit to Dublin. This time the nationalists decided they would be more active. Maud, still using her own name, Maud Gonne, summoned activists to her home in Coulson Ave Rathgar.A huge rally was to be organised, they heard, by the Irish Party for the Rotunda Buildings. Maud, Griffith, Edward Martyn, the Daughters of Erin and Cumann na nGael decided to infiltrate the rally and demand to know if there indeed was to be an official welcome for the King by the City. Protected by their own followers, but heavily outnumbered in the hall, Maud, Griffith and Martyn forced their way on to the platform where John Redmond and Tim Harrington sat. Maud demanded to know if they planned to welcome the King to Dublin. Unionist and Irish Party supporters rushed the stage and a riot broke out. Maud was lifted bodily to safety, much to her disgust. The riot received wide coverage with everyone noting the prominent role played by Miss Gonne. Shortly afterwards the Corporation voted not to welcome the King. Yeats joined in as before, with a letter to the newspapers repudiating the King's visit.

Pope Leo XIII died while the King was in Dublin. Maud insisted in flying a black flag of mourning at her own house, instead of the almost obligatory Union flag. Her neighbors objected. The police were called. Maud sent word to her own supporters who came and prevented the police removing the offending black flag.

Against the advice of other Board members, including Maud, Yeats decided to produce John Milligton Synge's first play – *In*

---

[72] . Fred Allan Collection .Manuscript 29817 NLI.

The Shadow of the Glen - that summer. The play was very controversial in that it was very realistic and portrayed the Irish peasant in a way most nationalists were not ready for. Maud resigned, from the Board. She had attended the opening night in the Molesworth Hall and to Yeats' bitter embarrassment staged a dramatic walk out mid-way through the performance. Griffith said Irish theatre should show Irish people in a good light and certainly not ridicule them as Synge had done. Maud tried to be somewhat diplomatic and wrote that outside influences often affected Irish writers for the worse. Though naming Yeats as the greatest living Irish poet, he too like Synge, because they lived so much outside Ireland were difficult to understand and appreciate, she said. Yeats was much wounded but luckily for him a change of scene beckoned, as he was shortly to leave for a literary lecture tour of the U.S.A. although he was to find that the controversy followed him. The *Irish Freedom* newspaper writing of his visit to the U.S.A. said, *"Mr. Yeats said that as soon as England saw a man of any intellect in Ireland, she missed no opportunity of bribing him to turn him away from the service of his country. One is now inclined to ask oneself if Mr. Yeats has accepted the bribe. We don't believe he has. But he could not render better service to England than at present, if he had accepted a thousand bribes. He has boasted of his 'moral victories' over the 'ignoramuses' of Clanna Gael. But he will find that his victories are in reality defeats"*.

John MacBride knew well of the very long and close relationship which existed between Millevoye and Maud. He presumed that Iseult resulted from their union, though Maud always referred to her officially as her adopted daughter. MacBride had some grudging respect for Millevoye as a man of the world like himself. But he had no such feeling for Willie Yeats or his passion for his wife. MacBride was not interested in poetry or poets. He despised Yeats and wished him out of his life and that of the National Movement. Shortly before the birth of their son MacBride wrote a letter to John Daly of Limerick, a mutual friend of his and Maud's. It read;

13 Rue de Passy
Paris
5/2/1903
My Dear Daly,

Mrs. MacBride wrote to Cassie after we got fixed in here asking her to come round and see us but we imagine she must have not received the letter, as we have not seen or heard from her. Would you send her our address. I am anxious to hear that delicious Limerick brogue of hers again.

Glad weeping William has retired into solitude he so richly deserves and from which he should never have emerged. He has set a good example to the other sprouting patriots.

Had a letter from Tom Clarke a few weeks ago. I suppose you receive The Gaelic American. It is very good and was badly needed in the United States. Tom is a brick.

If you are ever around Anthony MacRay shake him by the hand for me.

Best Wishes to all Limerick Friends
Slan leat, Old Man
Yours Ever
John MacBride [73]".

Maud had returned to Paris five months pregnant from Dublin. At the age of thirty seven, she had been through many public and private crises. The latter type always takes the most toll of the human spirit. She already had two children by a man who did not live up to her expectations. She had refused Willie Yeats's hand in marriage and many others. When she did marry and try and be a conformist, the results were disastrous; a husband she could not tolerate. But she still had a lot of loving to give and she wanted desperately to do so. That was why she was utterly happy as she came to full term. She knew it had to be a boy, someone who would love her and whom she could also love, like her dear father Tommy. There was no doubt in her mind that it would be so as it

---

[73] .Boer War to Easter Rising pp.97-8.

93

was in the stars and she was a good Catholic. Her baby boy was delivered safely in Paris on 26/1/I904. Messages of congratulations flowed in from all over the Irish world. A son had been born to an Irish Queen and her Hero Prince.

Maud placed the start of her husband's drinking to this time. She wrote:

After the birth of Sean I spent my time between Paris and Dublin. We had a house in Passy and John worked as Secretary to Victor Collins who earned a large salary as correspondent to the New York Sun and Laffan's Bureau, a fairly important news agency in New York. Despite my warning John became the inseparable companion of Collins, who introduced him to a rather undesirable drinking set who usually foregathered in the American Bar. He had an unhappy life in Paris. He did not know a word of French and must often have been very lonely, as my work kept me much in Ireland. I used to come over to Ireland leaving the children in the care of my good friend Mme. Avril de Sainte Croix. Sometimes I left Iseult in the convent at Laval where her godmother was the Superior[74].

---

[74] . Bureau of Military History. Statement of Maud Gonne MacBride 1949.

Maud, baby Seaghan, John MacBride.

A formal family photograph with - Jean Seagan MacBride - the flag of the Daughters of Ireland was prominent along with the Major's guns and sword, presented to him by John O'Leary. Posing for a formal picture though, neither parent looked at all happy, almost afraid of any eye contact occurring between them. For the first time in her life Maud was literally afraid of another human being. But her happiness was unbounded. At last she was a mother and could tell the world.

Maud decided to take her baby son to Ireland for baptism knowing the Major wouldn't be able to travel for fear of being arrested for his activities in the Boer War. They invited the frail John O'Leary to be Godfather. This caused difficulties at the Church in Terenure as O'Leary was not a Catholic. The MacBride family from Westport travelled up for the occasion. It was a public statement by Maud to all her many critics and detractors that she had gone legitimate. The police made a detailed report on all the proceedings including a list of the subversives attending. Maud would have preferred to live in Ireland but as her husband couldn't, the family home had to remain in France. John decided to go to America for several months at this period.

It was at this baptism in April 1904 that Joseph MacBride again met Eileen Wilson, Maud's half-sister/daughter. They fell in love and were married in London on 3 August that same summer. The marriage was a most successful one.

A few months later Maud returned alone to London to participate with John O'Leary in the Annual '98 Celebrations. Yeats though in London also didn't attend and didn't meet Maud. He was still annoyed with her for walking out of the Synge Play. Since he had recently been presented to the Queen, he was also slightly worried about what Maud's reaction would be. She had written him a letter from Paris objecting to his raising the prices at his Theatre, thereby putting it outside the reach of ordinary people. She reminded him that the revolution was meant to liberate all the people. A little later Maud arrived alone in Dublin and socialized with many of her old friends as Miss Gonne.

Maud wrote several times to John in America requesting that he return to Paris. He agreed to do so and arrived back at La Harve, where Maud collected him in August 1904. They went for a holiday at Maud's summer house in Coleville Normandy. There, to ease her husband's mind and to make a clean breast of matters, Maud confessed to the kind of life she had led with three different men; by one she had two children and two or three miscarriages. This had the opposite effect to what Maud had hoped for. It made John's mind up that he was leaving the marriage and returning to Ireland, where he would take his chances with the police.

Back in their Parisian home the domestic situation was deteriorating. McBride was jealous of his wife's freedom of movement, her access to the media and the well to do. He was becoming totally frustrated and resorting more and more to drinking with soldier comrades, coming home late at night disturbing the household. Maud resumed her journeys to Ireland in September taking baby Seaghan with her. John told her that she should leave the baby with his family in Westport as he intended to travel there shortly. But Maud returned to Paris in November with the baby. Maud travelled again to Ireland within a few weeks leaving the baby in Paris with John. When she announced the date of her return home, 25 November, John decided that he would travel to Ireland on that very date, accompanied by his friend Victor Collins, hoping that the police would never expect him to do so.

John left a letter for Maud to read on her return explaining his departure. He realized later that it was a very foolish letter to write. He said that their life was not a happy one due to her being unable to rise above a certain level. It was very painful for him to see that she was only a weak imitation of a weak man. He advised her that if he was executed or died in prison, she should remarry as she was a woman who could not live without some man or other behind her, even if she were a little unhappy, than to live an impure life[75].

Despite the objectionable letter they subsequently corresponded in friendly letters. On 15 December John wrote saying that he was going to Dublin and asked her to meet him there with the baby. Maud travelled to London with the baby and wired John in Westport that they would travel on to meet him in Dublin very shortly.

[75]. Fred Allan Collection Ms 29814 NLI

Chapter 12.

THE CUSTODY OF SEAN IS PARAMOUNT

Maud had feared that her husband might seek direct custody of the boy, which she could not contemplate as she saw her new baby as the re-incarnation of her dead baby Georges. In London she consulted a solicitor, Mr. Witham, the Gonne Trust solicitor, for advice in her situation. She then requested a meeting with her brother-in-law, Anthony MacBride, a London medical doctor, 'on a very important matter'. Anthony went immediately to May Clay's flat at 37 Alexandra Court, 171 Queen's Gate on Sunday 18th December. May met him first to tell him of Maud's alleged grievances concerning Iseult. Then Maud herself made a dramatic entrance and asked him to meet her at her solicitor's office the next day. At that meeting, Anthony was informed that a document was being drawn up for John's signature. In this he would admit to his guilt of an indecent offence against Iseult Gonne and give full control of Seaghan to Maud and immigrate permanently to America. Failure to sign would be followed by court action for criminal assault.

On that same night Anthony MacBride's wife set out for Dublin, where John was awaiting the arrival of his wife and child. The next morning Anthony's wife accompanied by Joseph MacBride, who had been summoned from Westport, met John on O'Connell Bridge. He had been on his way to attend the funeral of Arthur Griffith's father. John was most surprised. Anthony's wife informed him of the purpose of her visit. John was *'dumbfounded when I heard the charges formulated against me, but said immediately that I would start for London at once, see my wife and disprove the charges face to face'* [76].

The three arrived in London the next morning. John took a room at the Euston Hotel, where he was shortly joined by Anthony, *'accompanied by another nationalist caller'*. John's denial of the charge was not sought. He declared his intention of going directly to confront his wife but was persuaded to first consult the leading Irish nationalist lawyer, Barry O'Brien. John met O'Brien that same afternoon and informed him of the situation, as far as he knew it. O'Brien, who knew Maud quite well, was horrified that the matter would enter the public arena and damage the nationalist cause. He impressed upon John the absolute necessity of doing all to avoid this, without loss of honor. John agreed to be guided by O'Brien *'and the advice of a leader in the movement to which I belonged'*. Barry O'Brien asked John to get his brother, Anthony, to write to Maud inviting her to meet O'Brien the following morning. John informed O'Brien that for the past twelve months, he and Maud had not been together for more than three months. John wrote to Maud from the hotel after meeting O'Brien:

Euston Hotel 21-12-1904

My Dear Maud,
I learned on Tuesday last for the first time of the scandalous charges you and your English friends have been making against my character. They are absolutely false and of course I'll meet you and disprove them. I'd prefer not doing so publicly for little Seaghan's sake and yours: but I cannot lie under any such accusations, as I have been told you have been making lately. I can hardly credit you would believe the charges yourself. I went to Barry O'Brien today in order to consult him in the choice of a solicitor: but he suggested waiting until he had a talk with you. After you have seen Barry O'Brien please send me word saying where we can meet to talk matters over without any heat. I had to tell him who Iseult was. I said nothing otherwise. This is an awful blow to me as I was looking forward to a happy time in Ireland.

---

[76] . Ms. 29,818. NLI

Please make any arrangements so as to where I can see Seaghan each day while I am in London. Any place, any hour you name will suit me. His little happy face is always with me.

Your husband, John MacBride[77].

Maud did not reply to this letter.

Maud wrote to Barry O'Brien indicating that *'by Mr. Witham's advice I cannot receive my husband, also an interview between us would be very painful and quite useless.*
I would be grateful to you therefore if you would let him know three things which may influence his decision.
1st. That if you and Mr. Witham can arrange a separation giving me entire guardianship of Seaghan ... no one will hear of it from me.
2nd. If by getting work and leading a sober and decent life during seven years and proving he is worthy of it, I would not prevent him seeing Seaghan and having a share of his affection.
3rd. That if he forces me to put the French law into motion ... there are other certain things concerning his conduct during our married life which took place at my house and which if made public as they inevitably would be, would injure the reputation of a woman who I should think he has every reason to wish to spare. These things I only found out while inquiring into the other matter and it has been a great shock to me.
Please show this letter only to John, not even to Anthony'.

Maud met O'Brien as requested. He assured her that he was not taking sides in the matter and would not listen to charges and counter charges. His interest was that of Ireland and the avoidance of damaging publicity. Though he knew and liked Mr. Witham well, he had wished that the matter be confined to Irish people. But in the circumstance he felt that he had to deal with him as Maud had retained Mr. Witham. O'Brien told Maud that he was not acting for John in a legal capacity. When O'Brien and Witham met the following day, the latter informed

[77] Jordan Anthony J. *The Yeats Gonne MacBride Triangle.* Westport 2000. Pp 57-8.

him that he had hired detectives to guard against the kidnapping of Seaghan in London. They discussed a possible separation agreement, now that both parties had agreed to separate. Witham undertook to produce a draft agreement for MacBride's signature. When this was furnished, it stated that the boy would be under the sole and entire charge of the mother until aged ten. He would be reared a Catholic in a nationalist atmosphere, spending nine months each year in Ireland, unless ill or the husband interferes. The father could visit the boy once monthly and would renounce all rights to his wife's property.

Differences of interpretation would be adjudicated by Witham and O'Brien. When aged ten, adjudication would be made by nominated Catholic nationalists. In the event of death of both parents, the nominated Catholic nationalists would have guardianship.

Major MacBride responded to O'Brien immediately on receipt of the draft agreement. He proposed that the child should live with its mother for six years and the custody be opened 'de novo'. He suggested John O'Leary, a common friend to both, might act as arbitrator, with Cardinal Logue or Archbishop Walsh of Dublin, for guardianship. Though O'Brien had made it clear to both parties that he was not interested in charges and countercharges, MacBride included such in his reply. *'My wife listened to charges against me and declined to see me when I hastened to London. I wrote to her and I called to see her to deal with the matter at once. She refused to answer my letter, she refused to see me, and without consulting a single Irish friend (as far as I know) she went to an Englishman to take steps against me ... strange conduct on the part of Maud Gonne towards John MacBride.*

I wish to see her no more ... she has shown me that she is dead to any sense of justice ... I think only of Ireland and of my little boy and wish to be guided mainly by considerations for both, in all I do in this unhappy affair'[78].

It must have been a dire Christmas for both parties in London as negotiations ceased for a few days. As Maud had refused to have any contact with John, this meant he had been unable to see his son since

---

[78] . ibid.

his arrival in London. Barry O'Brien intervened and sought agreement that Mrs. Clay would take Seaghan to his home, where John could see him. This visit occurred on New Year's Eve. To the surprise of O'Brien and the amazement of John, it was not Mrs. Clay who came with the baby, but rather Maud Gonne herself. In fact Mrs. Clay, who appears to have been most inimical towards John, refused to come. When John entered the room, Barry O'Brien and Mrs. O'Brien were present with Maud, her nurse and the baby. John took no notice of Maud but went directly to Seaghan. Barry O'Brien and Maud then left the room. After a long period, O'Brien returned to say that Maud expressed her regret for not seeing John earlier and not allowing him to see Seaghan when he called to Mrs. Clay's house. Maud now wished to speak to John. The latter indicated that he had no wish to speak with her but agreed to comply with her request.

Within a few minutes of their meeting, John and Maud were arguing over the charges and counter-charges and control of Seaghan. In particular John denied having kissed Eileen Wilson. Maud countered saying that he had kissed Eileen 'behind the door'. Maud told him that Iseult had made a complaint to Mme. Avril and that she had told her not to tell anyone. Barry O'Brien then asked that if the baby required any food he would get his wife to give it some milk. Maud replied that it was better not to interfere with the youngster's food, as he took milk mixed with lime water. She added that in any case she was going away immediately.

Barry O'Brien agreed that if the baby was not to be fed there, it had better be taken home. Maud walked slowly past John, drawing herself up to her full height as he bowed slightly without uttering a word. She had got close to the door, when she suddenly wheeled round stretching out her hand to him. John took her hand and she fell weeping on it. This was too much for his gravitas and he began to laugh. Then the pair kissed and Maud said: *'I love you now John, but will hate you before you go to bed tonight'*. John reasserted that the charges were damnably false and that he was surprised that she should believe the words of others in preference to his. She kissed him as he swore in the most solemn manner that there was no truth in the charges. Then Maud said: *'of course I know there was nothing between you and Eileen except kissing'*. John then replied: *'It's you yourself that got Eileen to kiss me first and there was never a word or thought of love between Eileen and myself'*. He then said to Maud: *'If you meet me tomorrow Maud, we can talk it over quietly, for when all is said and done, you and I can settle this matter quicker and better than outsiders'*. Maud hesitated at this proposal and promised that she would write to him that same night. She kissed him several times. Then John took the child from the nurse and placed him in his wife's arms. In a moment Maud returned the child to the nurse. She then flung her arms round John's neck for the last time and gave him a parting kiss[79].

John waited the next day, New Year's Day 1905, for the promised letter which did not arrive. He decided to write to her. He said: *'I'd like to impress upon you that we owe it to our country and that it is only doing our duty towards little Seaghan to come to an understanding'*. In fact Maud had written as promised to John on the previous night but had not sent it. A covering letter dated 1/1/1905, accompanied the promised letter, which read:

Mr. Dear John,
I cannot see you tomorrow. I have been through so much my nerves are so overstrained, I should only break down foolishly as I did today. I do not, I cannot believe what you say. Mr. O'Brien will see Mr. Witham and draw up the terms of separation, the draft of which they will send me to Paris. I will write to you to Dublin news of Seaghan. What do you want me to do about all your things in Paris? Shall I send them to Dublin or Westport?
It is a sad New Year's Eve for us both. The years have been sad ever since our marriage. I hope the future may be more peaceful for both.

Seaghan's Mother.

Maud's decisiveness was again evident that same night as she also wrote to Barry O'Brien. It is clear that she was taken aback by her

---

[79] . Fred Allan Collection MS 29817 NLI

emotional display of the day and decided that she had better make her position clear.

'My Dear Mr. O'Brien,

I didn't thank you this afternoon as I should for your kindness, but I was rather upset. My nerves have been terribly overstrained lately, and seeing my husband the first time since I heard these terrible things was very trying. I would like to have believed all he said. I cannot do so. In the arrangements which you will make with Mr. Witham, it is useless to ask me to agree to anything less than ten years entire control of the child. I have already conceded too much - also I cannot allow nine months to be definitely defined for the child's time of residence in Ireland.

As I explained - it is and always has been, my intention to have Seagan brought up there; but I will not have a definite time laid down, by which should circumstances arise, make it inconvenient or impossible for me to do so. I will be open to be tormented and to have the whole question brought up again.

I am writing this to Mr. Witham who will send me the draft of the agreement to Paris where I go on Monday.

Please give my kind regards to Mrs. O'Brien and thank her.

Very sincerely yours

Maud Gonne MacBride.

1 Jan 1905

P.S.

I open my letter to add that it is obviously impossible to agree to John's proposal of seeing the child continuously ... It has occurred to me that he

might think of following me to Paris with the hope of getting me to give up separation. The house is in both our names. I could not legally refuse him admittance but I will not see him again.

If John keeps from drink and does not otherwise annoy me, I am not selfish and would gladly increase the opportunities for him to see the child, but it must be left to my discretion. I must have safeguards. You know Ireland and you know how terribly it will injure me, this separation without explanation. Both living in the same town will

make things far worse - and it always the woman who suffers in these cases ... If he were wise or wished really to atone for the wrong he has done, he would accept your suggestion of getting a commission in the American army. Apart from this, Dublin is about the worst place he could be in from the drink point of view. I don't believe he will get work there, at all events for a long time.
Maud Gonne MacBride'.

When O'Brien showed this letter to MacBride, he replied: *'It is not the woman who always suffers in these cases, but in this case the woman deserves to suffer. She was incapable of rising above the level of a second rate French mistress. The charges she proffered against me have no foundation except in her own diseased brain and the diseased brains of her friends'.*

MacBride agreed that Maud had broken down at their meeting but said the first advance had come from her. He admitted that he had met her half-way. He realized that this was weakness, but *'Adam Like'*, on his part saying: *'I will only add that I sincerely hope that I have now seen the last of this dramatic lady'.* He told O'Brien that Maud would never rear Seaghan away from Ireland: *'I would prefer to see him dead'.*

On that same New Year's Day, O'Brien, whose main interest remained avoiding a public scandal, fearing that Maud would return to Paris immediately wrote directly:
'Dear Mrs. MacBride,
I think that both you and your husband should remain in London for the
present. Take care you do not allow yourself to be dominated by English political family influences in a matter where the interests of your country are concerned.
This is no ordinary case of differences between husband and wife. Were it so the charges and countercharges made by you and your husband against each other would call for no interference from me. But this is a case where Irish national considerations must be taken into account. Therefore I cannot regard with indifference the prospect

of seeing you and your husband made the subjects of ridicule and contempt by the press of this country.

You are bound to think of the Irish cause with which you have been for so many years associated. Those who undertake public duties have public obligation. Your husband recognizes this fact. You will recognize it too if you are true to Ireland.

Yours Very Truly

R. Barry O'Brien   *100 Sinclair Rd West Kensington*[80].

Maud returned to Paris almost immediately. On 6 January she wrote, to John from Paris:

'My Dear John,

I am sending you one box containing the things mentioned in enclosed list.

I hat box containing five hats and a ring case with the ring Nally gave you which I dare say you would like to keep. 1 parcel containing 3 sticks.

I am having a case made for your addresses and several big pictures of yours. Shall I send them also to Barry's Hotel?

I have collected all the letters with American postmarks and put them together with your album and your writing book which is also full of papers. These I will keep with sword, sight of cannon and other souvenirs of the war until I get a suitable occasion of getting them safely delivered to you. If I let my house immediately, as is possible, I will get Mrs. Collins to take charge of them all unless you direct otherwise. Seaghan is very well. He slept the greatest part of the journey and was none the worse.

Maud Gonne MacBride

P.S. I am forwarding some letters but am keeping all American ones till I hear where to send them.

There are some wedding presents given by your family such as Beleek tea and coffee set, which belong to you, but the difficulty of sending them is great! I will try and send if you wish'.

---

[80]. MS. 29,814. NLI.

One can only imagine the reaction of MacBride on receipt of such a letter from his wife, who could scarcely wait to rid herself of his goods. However he retained his dignity, while replying frostily:

'Major John MacBride to Madame Gonne MacBride
Barry's Hotel 9.01.05
I beg to acknowledge receipt of yours dated 6 Jan and regret that having my things sent to Dublin should cause you so much trouble.
I am sure Mr. Collins will not object to take charge of any letters etc. you may give him for me.
It is not necessary to trouble about the wedding gifts just now as I have not a home ready for them at present.
Glad to learn that Seaghan was none the worse after his wanderings.
If you would kindly give instructions to have all my letters American and otherwise sent to above address, you would oblige.
John MacBride'.

The difference between John and Maud over the custody of Seaghan could not be bridged, though negotiations continued. Mr. Witham advised her that her husband grasped at every concession, using them to get new terms. He advised her to get some friend she could trust, to go over the whole thing with her and to decide on a firm course of action. It was at this stage that Maud, once again decided to turn to Willie Yeats. He had been in Dublin for the opening of a new season of plays, in what he regarded as his theatre, the Abbey. The Abbey was featuring plays of the three Directors, Gregory's, Synge's and Yeats'. The most difficult of the Irish nationalists, including Maud Gonne, had been disposed of. Willie was embarked on theatre for art's sake. His patron, Miss Horniman, who hoped to create an Irish Bayreuth at the Abbey, was still infatuated with him and had hopes of 'capturing' his hand in marriage. He was quite willing to play her along, while she provided the money and he could run the theatre his way.

Yeats lost no time in coming to Maud's help. He wrote immediately to Paris offering to be with her during her ordeal. She declined this generous offer telling him that *'it will be better for you not to come to Paris'*. She explained that John was insinuating that every male friend of hers was a lover. This information came to her, she told Yeats, via Barry O'Brien. She told Willie that MacBride had threatened to kill him. Willie's reaction to this information was to make a joke of it to Lady Gregory, describing it as the only cheerful news he had had in several days, adding that it added to the zest of life. Maud excoriated her husband to Yeats as a man *'without honor or scruples'*, sheltering behind the cause of Ireland. Though she did concede that his fidelity to that cause was true and genuine. She asked Willie to intervene with Barry O'Brien, whom she thought was over influenced by John. She included a copy of Mr. Witham's last letter to O'Brien. This in effect was an ultimatum to MacBride to accept the terms on offer or else face legal proceedings. It said that *'Mrs. MacBride will agree to no alterations at all in the terms. I will treat them as open for acceptance until Saturday. After that please consider them as withdrawn'*[81] . Yeats was well acquainted with Barry O'Brien. In 1901 Yeats had offered his resignation to the Irish Literary Society, in deference to Barry O'Brien, who would not allow Yeats' nomination of George Moore, as a member of the society, to proceed.

Willie Yeats was distraught by the sad news from Paris. His hatred towards MacBride grew even greater. As was his custom, he turned first to Lady Gregory to tell her the story, but also to seek her advice. He told her that he could not bear the burden alone and he knew nothing about the law. Acknowledging the hurt caused by Maud, he said that despite all that, when the details of the story are clear, no one could remain detached and unhelpful. Because it was clear to all his friends and colleagues that MacBride was totally dedicated to Ireland, Maud intimated to Yeats that it was going to be difficult, if it proved necessary in the end, to get witnesses to testify against him. Willie felt that Maud should not negotiate an agreement with MacBride but press ahead for a divorce. He realized that his own name could be dragged into the affair but was willing to accept, if not welcome that. She asked his advice on the possibility of getting witnesses to testify. He and Lady Gregory began to consider this aspect of the matter. Though they were closely involved in Irish affairs, many of their associates were not advanced nationalists and might prove useful in the

---

[81] . Ms. 29,817. NLI.

forthcoming battle. Willie told Lady Gregory that he had *'what is perhaps a wild project'* for spiriting MacBride out of the country and he wanted to discuss it with her in Dublin.

Maud also took her case directly to the advanced nationalists in Dublin, who were rallying around MacBride. She wrote directly to John O'Leary on 9.1.1905. He had earlier been mentor to her and to Yeats. She made it clear that unless John MacBride accepted the terms of separation, a scandal was inevitable. She told O'Leary that she was intent on living in Dublin. She ended her letter by saying *'Your Godson is beginning to walk'*. O'Leary was very perturbed by the situation, being so close to all parties. He replied immediately:

'17 Temple St Dublin 13/1/05
'My Dear Mrs. Gonne MacBride,
Knowing your husband as I do, I cannot believe that he has ever done anything that would make it impossible for you to live together, but whatever he has done, or whatever you think he has done, is a matter which as far as I can at all see, need not enter into the question of separation at all'.
Since both of them wanted to separate, O'Leary thought it should be straightforward, *'save for the terms of the boy's custody ... As to going into law, it would be a great scandal to all your friends ... such a course would be simply disastrous to yourself and no doubt extremely painful to your husband'[82].*

Maud also wrote to John's mother in Westport;

'My Dear Mother:
I am sorry for the pain this sad affair must give you. I have gone through so much sorrow since I married, especially since I found out everything, that I know what you must be suffering and I wish with all my heart I could spare it you, for no one deserves sorrow less than you do.
I have made no false accusations against John. I want to avoid bitter words so I will say no more on this point.

---

[82] . ibid.

Drink is I think responsible for everything. John has had terrible bouts of drinking at different times since our marriage. I had never before been in contact with a drunken man and no one will ever know what I suffered both before and after the birth of my child. When John is drinking he is mad. I tried to hide it all and told no one

This winter things came to my knowledge which made life together impossible. My first thought was to avoid scandal ... This lawyer and Barry O'Brien tried to arrange but failed as John, after all he had done had the pretension of posing conditions to me, whose married life has been blameless.

My lawyer told me he could do no more, so I returned to France and have begun proceedings for divorce ... If John is wise, even now, the divorce may be pronounced quietly and no one know the facts. I will do my utmost to avoid more scandal than is necessary.

I do not know what the cutting from the American paper may say. I have not seen it ... had it from Mr. Collins.

I have told no one any details except three members of my own family, my lawyers and the people directly mixed up in the affair, either here or in Ireland or London.

I am so sorry you have been ill and I am sorry I cannot say anything in this letter which will comfort you.

Little Seaghan is very well: he cut his 7th tooth yesterday: he is such a big boy now. He sends you his little wet kisses. He eats his soup every day with the spoon you gave him.

> *I am, dear Mother,*
> *Yours affectionately,*
> *(sad) Maud Gonne MacBride.*

This letter was again clearly intended to put pressure on John to settle the matter on Maud's terms or else face public proceedings.

It would appear that it was only when Maud returned from her two October-November visits to Ireland that the complaints against her husband were first made known to Maud. She had told Barry O'Brien in London that it was only after her marriage that she saw any signs of drink on John. It seems that her household members were frightened

110

by MacBride and his friends while she was away and made complaints to her. Whether these latter events were coincidental in Maud taking legal advice in London or whether they were the cause of it remains unclear. John and his friends believed that since he decided to live in Ireland, Maud became fearful about the custody of Seaghan and decided to take pre-emptive action.

Barry O'Brien showed MacBride Mr. Witham's last letter with Maud's final terms. After MacBride indicated that he would not accept any ultimatum from Maud, O'Brien wrote to Witham that he could do no more in the matter. He could not advise MacBride to accept the terms of separation. He included a veiled threat to Maud to the effect, that MacBride reserved the right to raise matters concerning her earlier life, should court proceedings ensue. These included some details of her past life that she had confessed to John on his return from America, *"that she had been the mistress to three different men. By one she had two illegitimate children and two or three miscarriages. By the others she had no children"*[83] And so all negotiations ended. Barry O'Brien advised John to make copies of all correspondence and documents relevant to the case in a book for future reference. O'Brien confirmed to Yeats that indeed MacBride had not accepted his wife's terms. Yeats was critical of what he regarded as O'Brien's tendency to favor MacBride.

Willie and Lady Gregory then decided to seek derogatory evidence against John MacBride in America. He had spent quite some time out there and people might feel freer to give evidence from that distance, rather than from Ireland. They decided to contact a mutual friend, the Irish American lawyer, John Quinn, who hired a private detective agency to carry out investigations. Willie told Quinn that MacBride *'has been a drunken cad from the first'*. He bemoaned the fact to Gregory that by becoming a Catholic, Maud had accepted Catholic values and codes, which were very deficient, especially where a woman's rights were concerned. He hoped that Maud might become the focus for improving the status of women in Ireland, thus removing her from extreme nationalism. Gregory agreed that the lot of women

---

[83] . Jordan Anthony J. *The Gonne Yeats MacBride Triangle* Westport Books 2000 p.52.

needed improving, but told Willie that she believed the probability of Maud being to able do any more work in Ireland 'is over for her'.

John Quinn succeeded in getting a negative affidavit from Maire Quinn, an actress who knew MacBride while he was in America. A Major Fritz Joubert Duquesne, an officer late of the EAR from South Africa also swore a negative affidavit though this was negatived by Louis Botha JJ Smuts and NJ deWet who swore *'We declare that we do not know such a person and as far as we know no one of that name was an officer of the EAR'*. Affidavits for MacBride came from Patrick Daly a member of Dublin Corporation, solicitor Henry Dixon and Gerald Ewing an opera singer. The most surprising pro-MacBride affidavit came from Jenny Wyse Power, an intimate of Maud Gonne's and a Vice-President of her Daughters of Erin. It read:

1. 'Jenny Wyse Power of 21 Henry St., Dublin, have been associated with Mrs. Maude Gonne-MacBride in Irish National Associations, particularly Daughters of Erin, of which she was President and I Vice-President in 1900-01.
2. After her marriage I never knew her to speak in any but the most affectionate terms of her husband. In November 1904 I spent a week as her guest in her house 26 Coulson Ave, Rathgar staying with her overnight. During this time she frequently spoke of her husband in a manner that led me to believe that the utmost confidence and affection existed between them. She expressed herself in continual dread least he might disregard the advice of his friends and come to Ireland and be arrested. She spoke of his restless state of mind in Paris and his passionate desire to return to his native country which she feared might lead him into serious danger and on several occasions she related to me how her sleep had been troubled by dreams in which her husband appeared in imminent peril. During my visits the most confidential relations existed between us and I was astonished when I heard some weeks later that she was making serious charges against her husband.
3. I was present at the christening of the child of the parties to this suit and on that occasion at Mrs. MacBride's house I met Joseph

MacBride and the lady to whom he was about to be married, Miss Eileen Wilson.

The relations between the latter and the petitioner appeared to me to be most cordial and I have personal knowledge of the fact that on the occasion of the wedding of Mr. and Mrs. Joseph MacBride the petitioner presented the bride with a trousseau.

4. I have met the respondent Major John MacBride frequently since his return to Ireland. I have never seen him under the influence of drink nor have I known him to ever conduct himself otherwise than as a well-bred gentleman.

Sworn 18 November 1905 [84].

 *John Quinn*

It was from Yeats that Maud first heard of Barry O'Brien's confirmation that MacBride was indeed not going to accept her terms. She then saw a judicial separation or a divorce as the options to render her complete security for the control of the child. She had already retained a French lawyer, a Mr. DeTroy, and given him a statement. He advised her that she had sufficient evidence against her husband without using the alleged assault against Iseult. Maud asked Willie to advise her about engaging an Irish barrister to counter MacBride's criticisms about her engaging an English lawyer. She asked him to get Mrs. Clay to discuss it with Mr Witham. While Maud expressed her heartfelt thanks to Willie for his support and sympathy, she was insistent that she did not want him getting drawn into *'this horrible*

---

[84] . *Yeats Gonne MacBride Triangle* pp. 86-7.

affair'. She had brought it on her own head and must see it through herself.

Mr. Witham's advice had been less satisfying, though very clear. On 16 January he told Maud that she should ask M. Detroye to get accurate statements from her witnesses. Witham told her that if they could prove in court what those witnesses said, she would get her separation and custody of Seaghan. He advised her that the courts did not take any notice of drunkenness, unless *'a man knocks his wife about when he is drunk'*[85]. He said that if she intended to live in France, a French divorce might suffice. But since she intended to travel to England and Ireland, it was essential that she procure a separation in England.

In Ireland John MacBride was rallying support among his own friends. Arthur Griffith and Henry Dixon approached Maud's own group, Inghinidhe na hEireann, offering to mediate. John also wrote to several French friends asking them to intervene. Maud rebuffed all approaches at mediation. One of these was from Suzanne Foucart, Iseult's godmother, in whose convent Iseult and Eileen Wilson sometimes stayed while Maud was travelling. She replied to John on 17 January apologizing for the delay. She sympathized and hoped that *'things won't go that far, but that you will finish by reaching an agreement with Maud and that your home will be once again united and happy'*. On 2 February John was asked to deliver a lecture in Cork for the O'Donovan Rossa Fund. While agreeing in principle, he advised *'do not advertise me as going down as I cannot make any definite arrangements until I have some private business fixed up'*[86]. George Russel and Ella Young, as the Berg Collection in the New York Public Library makes clear, also expressed their wish to arbitrate between the couple. Yeats was not amused and was in conflict with Russell on the matter.

Yeats' advice to Maud was that a decision in court was the best way of vindicating her position. She was further decided on this course by

---

[85] .ibid.
[86] . Jordan Anthony J. *Major John MacBride*. Westport Historical Society 1991. p. 69.

the knowledge that such cases were held in camera, with the verdict alone publicized. Her French lawyer advised that her case must be strong enough to satisfy English law too, lest any complications arise in that jurisdiction in the future. To ensure that, he insisted that Maud's charges involving Eileen Wilson be included, though she hoped not to have to use them. She realized that the other evidence, particularly that of her friends and employees, was weak, but she hoped it would be corroborative. She realized that the case could take as long as six months to process. She confided in Willie that she knew her husband was putting it about that her mind *'was unhinged'*[87] One of MacBride's supporters, Victor Collins, was suspected by Maud of giving the story of the impending separation to *The New York World*. Maud told Willie that she believed this was the first public announcement of the affair.

---

[87]. Gonne Yeats Letters p.189.

Chapter 13.

DIVORCE CASE AND VERDICT

On 3 February 1905 Maud made her written legal petition. The document reads:

Mrs. Edith Gonne, wife of Mr. John MacBride, without profession, having Mr. Detroye for Attorney, married on 21 February 1903 in Paris at the English Consulate, married without any contract that in accordance with the terms of the English Law, Mr. and Mrs. MacBride are married under the regime of the separation of goods. That only one child has been born of the marriage, a little boy now aged one year.

That the petitioner was not long in suffering from the jealous, suspicious and violent temper of her husband, that his intemperate habits, his unbridled licentiousness and his unscrupulous immorality constitute a dangerous environment for the petitioner and rendered life with him insupportable.

That in consequence Mrs. MacBride is obliged to sue for a divorce from Mr. MacBride[88]

The hearing was before the Civil Tribunal of the Seine. MacBride's lawyer denied that his client was a rake as described by the opposing lawyer. He admitted that his client was then a heavy drinker. He also claimed that MacBride had a large input into his wife's journalistic output. He insisted that Maud was an English woman with no familial connections to Ireland. To the horror of the MacBride family, Maud felt obliged to accuse her husband of committing adultery with her

---

[88] .Yeats-Gonne-MacBride Triangle p. 71.

half-sister/daughter Eileen Wilson, prior to her marriage to Joseph MacBride.She hoped that such a move would force John MacBride to submit to her demands. Eileen Wilson had never been acknowledged by Maud for who she was. Eileen travelled from Westport with her husband to refute the allegation and the Court accepted her evidence. Maud had decided not to include the alleged molesting of her daughter Iseult in court, no doubt to protect her from having to give evidence in court. In the event Dr. Anthony MacBride insisted on raising it, to clear John's name. This was a dangerous tactic as if accepted by the Court, John would face a long prison sentence for such an offence. Many witnesses gave evidence for each party. As the case dragged through the Courts, the final verdict came on 8 August 1906. Its final conclusions read:

Judgement
Du Tribunal Civil de La Seine
Le 8 Aout 1906
Entre Madame MacBride
Pemanderene au principal
D'efonderesse reconventionnel

Et M. MacBride,

D'e efendeur au principal.
Dermadeur reconventionnet

Le Tribunal, oui
Enlaurs conclusions et liadoiriers
Crippi, avocet, assiste de Detroye.
Aroue dela dame MacBride;
Labori, avocet, assiste de Goirand avoune John MacBride

Judgement of the Civil Tribunal of the Seine
8 August 1906
Regarding the Petition for divorce brought by Mrs MacBride:

Given that Mr. MacBride is an Irish subject who has always kept his nationality; that if at a certain time he left Ireland to go first to the Transvaal and then to France, there is no evidence to show that he gave up his nationality or that he gave up any idea of returning to his country.

On the contrary, given that his marriage to the plaintiff was celebrated in France, not before an official of the French State but before the English Consul and that the baptism of the child of that marriage, born in Paris, was held in Ireland;

That MacBride, contrary to the allegations of his wife, never intended to settle in France

That certificates to this effect were given to the court; firstly, that the English wife by entering a marriage with an Irishman acquires the personal status of the latter;

Secondly, English law which allows divorce is not recognised in Ireland whose courts cannot grant divorce between Irish subjects and only separation 'a mensa et thoro' which is similar to separation in French civil law;

Given that the suit brought by Mrs. MacBride with regard to divorce is not permissible, she should be considered as entitled to obtain a Separation which is the only recourse allowed by the national law of the couple.

Regarding Mrs. MacBride's case;

Given that the case of immorality attributed to Mr. MacBride has not been sufficiently established.

But, from evidence and testimony of the second, third, fifth, sixth, seventh, eight, tenth, twelfth and thirteenth witnesses for the inquiry; seventh, eleventh, and twelfth for the counter claim, that the habits of intemperance (drunkenness) of MacBride is evident.

That their public status, especially their education and social position allows Mrs. MacBride to regard them as constituting a serious injury which justifies the case.

Regarding Mr. MacBride's case:

Given that Mr. MacBride in support of his counter claim for Separation, puts forward only the serious injury that his wife has inflicted on him by accusing him of immorality;

But given that he has not established that these claims were made in bad faith and in order to defame him, they would not be considered as constituting a serious injury to him.

Regarding Custody of the child;
Custody granted to the mother with visiting rights granted to the father to be decided later.
For these reasons:
Divorce not granted as requested by Mrs. MacBride for reasons of the nationality of the couple. However separation granted with all the consequences of the law in favor of Mrs. MacBride, Mr. MacBride's counter claim denied.
Given that separation involves separation of property, the President of the Chamber directs the lawyers to commence winding up the couple's estate. He directs M. Rene Petit, judge, to make his report and approval.

Custody of the child granted to the mother. If the parents are unable to settle visiting rights of the father, the latter will have the right to visits to his home from the child, while he is less than six years, escorted by his mother once a week on Mondays from one until four and that MacBride will escort him back to his mother. When the child has reached the age of six, the father may have the child to stay for one month from 1ˢᵗ - 31ˢᵗ August every year.

Costs against MacBride.

Maud gave a lengthy interview to the *New York Evening World*. She said
"If a woman has really something worthwhile to do in the world, I say unhesitatingly that marriage is a deplorable step. If she is an ordinary commonplace woman, then she might as well marry as not. No matter how loving her husband is when he first marries, a man is sure to become jealous or sarcastic about his wife's career. In the end he is likely to make his wife's life a living hell. In these days the woman is likely to be better educated than her husband. It

is a fatal error for such a woman to take on such a man.Then he makes another kind of hell by misunderstanding her and ridiculing her from the standpoint of his hopeless inferiority. I deny that marriage is the best arrangement possible". She added that if such a woman did marry and wished to pursue a career and earn money, and then it was perfectly alright for her to employ suitable help to look after the home and family. But she warned that in marriage, men found it difficult to play fair, so that many career women *"might just as well shun marriage"*[89].

This interview was poorly received when reported in Dublin. Maud made efforts to repudiate it, but she only served to create more sympathy for her husband. He had brought a suit against the *Irish Independent* in Dublin for defamation. This served to lengthen the notoriety of the case and recreated it in Ireland again. Maud wrote to Yeats, *"Nothing but madness can have prompted MacBride to take a libel case against the Independent for having published a much modified account of what took place in the Paris Courts"*[90]. He won his case but was awarded the derisory amount of £1. He remained on in Dublin, reckoning correctly that the Government would have little interest in pursuing him. He became a favorite drinking companion of John O'Leary, who had sided with him throughout the divorce proceedings. The Major had at least won freedom of movement for himself, as he tried to become part of a nationalist movement. Many people in Dublin believed he had been used as a pawn by Maud, and were very sympathetic to him and antagonistic to Maud.

Maud was still married legally and morally. Should she take her son to England or Ireland the Major could take custody of him. Her freedom of movement became limited. She had to resign herself to greater domesticity than she liked. She only spoke French to her son, so that even if her husband exercised his visiting rights, he would not be able to talk to him. MacBride did exercise his visiting rights on a few occasions before he returned to Dublin, never to see his son again. Some have

---

[89]. Major John MacBride p.76.
[90]. Gonne –Yeats Letters p. 228.

deemed Maud's action as an early episode example of *parent alienation syndrome*.

Maud was furious with the verdict and informed Willie that she would probably appeal, after first sacking her lawyer, Mr. Cruppi, whom she said *'neglected my affairs shockingly*[91].The verdict meant that should she take Seaghan to Ireland, John could legally claim him. The prospect having to live for the foreseeable future in France did not appeal to Maud.

Adrian Frazier ends his study of the issue thus, "In *MacBride's later life, all the way to his execution in 1916, there is nothing to show that he was either a serial child molester or an alcoholic. Even though her charges remained unproven in court, MacBride should have known better than to start a fight with Maud Gonne*"[92].

Maud wrote in her 1949 Statement to the Bureau of Military History: *After the birth of Sean I spent my time between Paris and Dublin. We had a house in Passy and John worked as Secretary to Victor Collins who earned a large salary as correspondent to the New York Sun and Laffan's Bureau, a fairly important news agency in New York. Despite my warning John became the inseparable companion of Collins, who introduced him to a rather undesirable drinking set who usually foregathered in the American Bar. He had an unhappy life in Paris. He did not know a word of French and must often have been very lonely, as my work kept me much in Ireland. I used to come over to Ireland leaving the children in the care of my good friend Mme. Avril de Sainte Croix. Sometimes I left Iseult in the convent at Laval where her godmother was the Superior.*

 My husband came back to Ireland, I think in 1906, when Sean was two years old. I was in Ireland and was summoned back to Paris by my friend, Mine. Avril de Ste. Croix to look after my house which was being sadly neglected and ill-used. On my arrival my friend told me that my husband had left Paris for Ireland with Victor Collins. Our trains must have crossed, she said. I thought he would be arrested straightaway, as Arthur Lynch was, for his part in the Boer War in the

[91] . ibid. p. 232

[92] .Frazier Adrian, *The Adulterous Muse,*The Lilliput Press 2016. p. 236.

Transvaal. Victor Collins, who had neglected his own work, had got the sack from his two papers. He got employment years later from Father Sweetman in his school in Gorey. I always thought he was the undoing of McBride. I got a legal separation shortly afterwards, having failed to get an amicable separation which would give me complete control of my son's upbringing[93].

After the verdict in Paris, John MacBride returned to Dublin where he decided to try and break into journalism. On 13 October he wrote to John Devoy: *'The Freeman is taking four or five articles from me on the Irish Brigade and I would be glad, if you would think it advisable, if the Gaelic American would insert them. I sent you the first which appeared today'*. MacBride then mentioned a possibility which Maud had earlier mentioned to Yeats, that because of all the bad publicity he might find it impossible to secure a decent job at home. Despite his good name in America he was realistic enough to know that it might not be politic for that paper to publish his material, despite the *Freeman's Journal* doing so. He told Devoy: *'You will understand though that if you consider it would be better for the G.A. not to touch them, or me, I will feel in no way hurt or offended'*[94].

Devoy did publish his articles, beginning in November. MacBride's introduction to those articles reads: *'It is now exactly seven years since the outbreak of the South African War and the details of that great struggle are, of course familiar to most of your readers. But with the permission of the Editor of this journal, I will try and set forth, as briefly as possible, some facts in connection with the formation of the Irish Brigade and the part taken by it in the campaign, which are scarcely likely to be generally known, and the knowledge of which, I cannot help thinking, should be welcomed by every liberty-loving son and daughter of a race whose renown for bravery and chivalry, dates from the time before history came to be set down in written permanent form*[95]. The *Freeman's Journal* eventually published thirteen articles from MacBride, between 13

---

[93] . Bureau Military History. Statement No.317.

[94] . Major John MacBride. P. 78-79.

[95] . ibid. p.78.

October 1906 and 29 July 1907. These remain valuable source material for the story of the Irish Brigade in the Boer War[96].

CHAPTER 14.

YEATS FINALLY MAKES LOVE WITH MAUD

The following year a play by Lady Gregory "*The Gaol Gate*" was being staged in Dublin. Maud attended accompanied by Willie Yeats. As they entered the Theatre together with Maud dressed in black, hissing started as she was recognized. Somebody shouted "*Up McBride*". A counter sound developed overpowering her detractors as more people realized what was happening. Willie was furious but Maud smiled regally as they took their seats. The future Mary Colum who witnessed the event wrote, *her whole figure showing a lively emotion, and I saw the most beautiful, the most heroic-looking human being I have ever seen before or since...She was a legend to us young persons in our teens".* "Yeats later wrote in "*Phoenix*" of the event, "*The drunkards, pilferers of public funds....*"[97].

Maud had a wide circle of friends in Paris where she could easily get involved. She began to devote herself to some of her own artistic pursuits, like painting. She was a passable portrait painter and an accomplished watercolor artist. She exhibited her work on a commercial basis. There were also various Irish societies where she was always a much sought after guest. Paris was a diverse city and Maud became particularly friendly with the exiled Indian Nationalist leader Madame Cama. She was also a prolific letter writer. She kept in close touch with her *Daughters of Erin*, through Helena Moloney, directing its affairs where possible. But things were changing in Dublin. Arthur Griffith founded a new paper called, *Sinn Fein (Ourselves Alone)*, which became aligned to the new party of the same name. Maud's own Parisian paper, *L'Irlande Libre* had ceased publication. The women in Dublin were becoming

---

[97] .Colum Mary *Life and the Dream* MacMilan 1947 p. 142

more radicalized, from a feminist and socialist point of view. They launched their own paper, "*Bean na hEireann* " (*Woman of Ireland*) which wanted to encourage women to become participants in nationalist affairs at every level. Maud became a regular contributer.The more radical of the women began to be influenced by James Connolly's socialist principles. Constance Marckievcz became an ardent socialist and physical force convert, leaving her child to be brought up by her own mother. Maud publicly defended her colleague's great sacrifice.

But during these years in Paris her life was really only made bearable by the devotion of Willie Yeats. Once again he crossed the Channel many times to stay nearby at the hotel at Passy. Maud began to tell him how he was in her dreams needing her support which she wanted to give but could not. In a letter of 26 July 1908 she wrote how he had *"evoked union"* with her.

"It is not a week but in a day that I am writing to you. I had such a wonderful experience last night that I must know at once if it affected you & how? Last night I thought I would go to you astrally...I put on this body & thought strongly of you & desired to go to you. We went somewhere in space...You had taken the form of a great serpent. I looked into your eyes and your lips touched mine. We melted into one another till we formed one being, a being greater than ourselves who felt all & knew all with double intensity- the clock striking 11 broke the spell & as we separated it felt as if life was being drawn away from me through my chest with almost physical pain. I went again twice, each time it was the same...Then I went upstairs to bed & I dreamed of you...We were quite happy, & we talked of this wonderful spiritual vision I have described - you said it would tend to increase physical desire - This troubles me a little, for there was noting physical in that union - Write to me quickly & tell me if you know anything of this & what you think of it & if I may come to you again like this. I shall not until I hear from you. My thoughts with you always"[98].

---

[98] . *Gonne-Yeats Letters* pp. 256-7.

It has generally been elucidated from Yeats' poetry *[Fallen Majesty- No Second Troy- Peace- Among the Reeds]* that some months later in December, the couple did engage in sexual intercourse, but that it was not successful. Adrian Frazier writes that *"Yeats discovered that the most beautiful woman he had ever seen was no longer quite so beautiful. Nothing could compare with the oft-imagined flesh of the muse; the uncovered body of a 42-year old mother of three disenchanted him"* [99]. Maud realized this and insisted that they return to a spiritual marriage and become spiritual lovers. Willie had been getting plenty of sexual release elsewhere with the actress Florence Farr and the masseuse Mabel Dickenson. He was becoming more mature and able to control his sexual passion for Maud. This was just as well as she was now introducing another element against their physical union, writing *"I have prayed so hard to have all earthly desire taken from my love for you...may be taken from you too"* She adverts to the fact of how rare a thing it is for a man to hold spiritual love when the bodily desire is gone.Willie wrote in his notebook:*"We are divided by her religious ideas, a Catholicism which has grown on her - she will not divorce her husband and marry because of her Church. Since she has said this, she has not been further from me but is always very near.She seems to love more than of old. In addition to this the old dread of physical love has awakened in her"*.

---

[99] . *The Adulterous Muse* Frazier Adrian, The Lilliput Press 2016. p. 244

But at the same time Maud felt positive about their astral relationship. She wrote to him in later 1909, *You asked me yesterday if I am not a little sad that things are as they are between us —I am sorry & I am glad. It is hard being away from each other so much there are moments when I am dreadfully lonely & long to be with you - one of these moments is on me now – but beloved I am glad and proud beyond measure of your love, & that it is strong enough & high enough to accept the spiritual love & union I offer.*

Their unique relationship was in the main carried out through letter writing over the next few years. Willie had his work through the theatre and poetry and sexual fulfillment though his mistresses. Maud's main concern was her children especially her son Seaghan, who became the main focus of her life.

A cause for argument between the astral lovers was Willie's continuing involvement in the theatre in Dublin. Maud felt he was devoting too much of his valuable time to such a difficult enterprise. She also knew of course that Lady Gregory was a full partner of his in it. *"Your true work is your poetry"* she said, *"Concentrate on that"*. She realized well that the public knew that she was his great inspiration in this field, and that it would also bring fame and immortality to herself. It would also keep him on her plane and she was coming to depend more and more on him. In praise of her he compared her to Helen of Troy when he wrote of her nobleness and beauty and potential.

NO SECOND TROY

Why should I blame her that she filled my days
With misery, or that she would of late
Have taught to ignorant men most violent ways
Or hurled the little streets upon the great,

Had they but courage equal to desire?
What could have made her peaceful with a mind
That nobleness made simple as a fire,
With beauty like a tightened bow
That is not natural in an age like this,
Being high and solitary and most stern?
Why, what could she have done, being what she is?
Was there another Troy for her to burn?

Maud went to the Courts again and was successful in having MacBride's right to have his son live with him for a month at a time later on, ended. The Appeal judge indicated that she was entitled to seek a divorce in France and invited to reapply in three years. She would have preferred to move to Ireland, now that Iseult was almost grown up and Seaghan ready for school. But she was still scared her husband might take the boy. One summer she summoned up enough courage and took all the family to Mullraney in County Mayo for a holiday. It was near the MacBride family home in Westport, where paradoxically she felt fairly safe. They visited the old Mrs. MacBride and got on very well with her and the whole family. Of course her own half-sister/daughter, Eileen, was married to Joseph MacBride since 1904, before any legal proceedings started. The terrible fact that in her Court proceedings Maud had alleged adultery between John MacBride and Eileen Wilson must still have galled enormously. John MacBride continued to live in Dublin and did not appear in Westport during Maud's visit. Willie Yeats paid them a fleeting visit from which came his second poem written to Iseult as a follow up to his earlier one. In it he warns her how difficult life can be and despite the evidence of how her mother suffered he feels Iseult because she is young will also be a victim.

TWO YEARS LATER

Has no one said those daring
Kind eyes should be more learned?
Or warned you how despairing
The moths are when they are burned?
I could have warned you; but you are young,
So we speak a different tongue.
O you will take whatever's offered
And dream that the entire world's a friend,
Suffer as your mother suffered,
Be as broken in the end.
But I am old and you are young,
And I speak a barbarous tongue.

Back home again in Paris Maud began to think again of becoming directly involved in Ireland. Ever since she had been connected with the Patriotic Children's Treat in the Phoenix Park, she knew how malnourished children were in Dublin. There was a *Schools Meals Act* in force in England whereby children got a dinner in school each day. Maud had raised the issue in *Bean na hEireann*, saying that the Act should be extended to Ireland. She decided to return to Ireland and fight this issue. She mobilized her own Daughters of Ireland. James Connolly and the Irish Trades Council joined her, Helena Moloney, Constance Markievcz, Kathleen Clarke, Sydney Gifford, and Hanna Sheehy-Skeflington worked on a committee. Maud approached a priest friend who managed schools in the Liberties area of the city and they started a pilot project feeding the children at school.

A Monster Meeting was held at the Mansion House resolving that Dublin Corporation should begin a free school meals service. A deputation, including Maud, went to London to see the Home Secretary, asking him to pass enabling legislation extending the Act to Ireland. Many or the Parish Priests opposed the scheme as they feared governmental intervention in their parochial schools. But gradually the voluntary scheme was extended pending the extension of the Act. This particular campaign though mainly successful, again made some enemies for Maud. Willie Yeats wrote that she carried on regardless. He said that it is not for praise she became involved. But the begrudgesrs will complain and tell lies about her though she is operating on a different plane.

Around this time in Dublin Maud met many of the current Nationalist leaders. She was very impressed with Padraig Pearse's school, St. Enda's in Rathfarnham, where Irish culture was a huge part of the curriculum. She was also introduced to a teacher there named Thomas MacDonagh, by Pearse himself. Both teachers were poets, MacDonagh having already had two books of his work published. She thought it would be a very fitting place for her son to be educated, it they could all return safely.

Maud's husband was also living in Dublin then, having joined the Irish Republican Brotherhood (I.R.B.), a secret revolutionary group. Maud was successful in assisting him in getting a job with Dublin Corporation as Water Bailiff, though he resented her interference greatly.The police Report said,
"This does not appear to have brought a reconciliation between them; on the contrary 'Major' MacBride is alleged to have resented her interference in the matter"[100]. MacBride received thirty-two out of the fifty-nine votes cast and was awarded the post in January 1911. Among his most ardent advocates were Councillor WT Cosgrave and Tom Kelly. Maud and John never communicated even though they passed each other in the street on a couple of occasions. It was most embarrassing for their mutual friends.

From Paris Maud had supported the Irish Women's Suffragette Movement and their opposition to the Dublin visit of King George V. But on the streets it was now Constance Marckievcz with James Connolly's socialists who were then in the vanguard of agitation. Their paper, *The Irish Citizen*, became widely read. The famous *1913 Lock-Out* in Dublin also saw Maud a spectator in France. For eight months

---

[100] .Police Report 20 Dec. 1910 National Archives Dublin.

100,000 Dublin workers were on the streets fighting for Union rights. In the end they had to go back to work but they had won a moral victory. The poverty and hardship it engendered was staggering in its scale. Maud, with Arthur Griffith, was unhappy, unlike Constance Marckievcz, at the development of a class war situation by union leaders like Jim Larkin, who lead the strike. Ile was too vain a man to be a national leader. When the strikers were forced back to work Maud decided she must return to Dublin to help in the aftermath. Most of the people had pawned all their belongings to buy food. Now they had to be assisted to redeem their tickets by people who could lay their hands on hard cash. Maud collected money quietly and privately for this purpose.

Willie Yeats was very disturbed by the episode and saw the bitter defeat of the Irish workers by the Irish merchants as a betrayal. Profit was the raision d'etre of commerce and the lot of the worker was secondary. This was not the country Yeats had striven to build. It was not for this that patriots like Lord Edward Fitzgerald, Robert Emmet,Wolfe Tone had given up their lives. He concluded sadly that like his and Maud's early mentor, John O'Leary, their ideal Ireland was dead.

SEPTEMBER 1913

What need you, being come to sense,
But fumble in a greasy till
And add the halfpence to the pence
And prayer to shiffering prayer, until
With some appropriate commentary on each;
Until imagination brought
A fitter welcome; but a thought
Of that late death took all my heart for speech.
You have dried the marrow from the bone?
For men were born to pray and save;
Romantic Ireland's dead and gone,

It's with O'Leary in the grave.

Was it for this the wild geese spread
The grey wing upon every tide;
For this that all that blood was shed,
For this lord Edward died,
And Robert Emmett and Wolfe Tone,
All that delirium of the brave?
Romantic Ireland's dead and gone,
It's with O'Leary in the grave.

On the political front Home Rule was being offered by the Government. In Ulster, Loyalists had set up their own army to oppose it. In the South too a Volunteer forces were established. The stage was being set for a civil war. Maud was on a recuperative holiday for all the family, including Helena Maloney in the Pyrenees. At this stage she was quite willing to accept Home Rule as a stepping stone to full Irish freedom. She remained in close touch with Willie who was now in receipt of a Government stipend as a help to his literary work, He was very pessimistic about the Irish situation believing the Ulster Volunteers to be more than a match for their southern opposition. He also felt that the South would be better off without *'those difficult Northerners'*.

But a greater war was already breaking out. Germany declared war on Russia and on France. It then invaded Belgium which forced England into the war. Irish Home Rule was postponed. The German army moved further westwards. Maud, Iseult, and Helena worked in a hospital near the Pyrenes for three months helping wounded soldiers. Eleven year old Seaghan was a page boy. The horror and futility of war soon became apparent to them as casualties mounted. They managed to get back to Paris from where they travelled to Normandy. She wrote to Willie in December 1914, " *We are back in Paris – after 3 months hard red cross nursing...I have no military enthusiasm...Paris is very sad and everyone seems to be in mourning*"[101]. Kathleen, Maud's sister, joined Maud after her eldest son was killed in action. Maud feared for her sister's sanity. Maud hoped that the war would make Iseult a less headstrong and moody girl. Maud was urging Irishmen not to get involved in the war. But in the first year 80,000 Irish joined up to fight for the freedom of small nations, as it was put by John Redmond. Maud was appalled at this betrayal of Ireland. Some in Ireland thought the same.

O'Donovan Rossa, the old Fenian died. His body was brought home to Glasnevin for a hero's funeral in 1915. At the graveside, the various private armies including Cumann na mBan, Connolly's Citizen Army, the Volunteers, heard P.H. Pearse deliver the oration to the thousands gathered. He ended by saying," *The fools, the fools, they have left us our Fenian Dead - and while Ireland holds these graves, Ireland unfree snail never be at peace".* Among those on the organizing committee were Eamon deValera, Thomas MacDonagh, Arthur Griffith, Joseph McGuinness, Cathal Brugha, Constance Markievicz, Thomas Clarke, Kathleen Clarke, Diarmaid Lynch, Cathal Brugha, William O'Brien and Major John MacBride. As Pearse spoke the man standing directly behind him was Major John MacBride.

AT THE GRAVESIDE

[101]. *Gonne –Yeats Letters* p, 352.

Chapter 15.

"MACBRIDE HAS BEEN SHOT"

Maud Gonne and Willie Yeats had confidently predicted that after the divorce case, there would be no future for John MacBride in the nationalist movement in Ireland. Yeats had written to Maud that, *"your husband will gradually sink and disappear now"*. Their predictions, and no doubt hopes, while very understandable, were to prove entirely wrong. Though MacBride was well aware that some might want to shun him, he never countenanced withdrawing from the national struggle. He became an integral and valued activist for the movement, which would lead eventually to the 1916 Rising. He retained his own self-confidence, and showed no fear of the authorities. He remained a highly active member of the IRB and was the focus of monthly police reports, from which his movements and activities are clearly discernible.

Early in 1907, MacBride and the nation, had suffered a blow, when John O'Leary died. For so very long, O'Leary had been the living symbol of resistance to English rule. He had played a vital role in the nationalist careers of Maud Gonne and Willie Yeats. The funeral took place to Glasnevin cemetery on a very wet public holiday Monday. It was not a large funeral, rather an indication of the poor organisational state of the IRB. Among those who carried the coffin was John MacBride. Though Willie Yeats was in Dublin, he did not attend. Two years later, a large Celtic cross was unveiled over the grave by the IRB, in the presence of Arthur Griffith, Fred Allen, PT Daly and John MacBride. The latter had become a much sought after public speaker at commemorative events. His most famous address occurred in Belfast in 1911 on the subject of Robert Emmett. When Winston

Churchill was being tutored on public speaking in New York by William Bourke Cockran they used the text of MacBride's speech[102].

The quest for Home Rule by the Irish Parliamentary Party had long been the dominant political matter in Ireland. But the emergence of Sinn Fein, out of Cumann na nGael, and its by election victory in North Leitrim in 1908, over the IPP, on an abstentions ticket, changed the political landscape. The arrival home from America of Tom Clarke, a very close friend of MacBride's, was also of crucial importance. However, the Sinn Fein decision to tone down its policies so as to give the IPP a clear run at the General Election of 1910, resulting in the IPP holding the balance of power at Westminster, did not find favor with the IRB or MacBride.

John MacBride fell in love with a lady named Clara Allan. She was the wife of Fred Allan a notable nationalist figure in Dublin. They were Quakers and lived in Glenageary and MacBride lived with them.

In 1912 MacBride receive a letter from Patrick Pearse which read:

" Sgoil Eanna
Rathfarnham
17 February
1912.
A Chara,
Could you find time to address the members of St. Enda's Branch of the Gaelic League in our Study Hall, some Friday evening in the near future? The subject of the address need not be immediately concerned with the work of the Gaelic League – any subject likely to appeal to the imagination of young Gaels would do; history, literature, science, travel, antiquities, industry, even politics in the wider sense, would all be admissible. Neither need the address be in Irish, for we masters and the older boys will see to it, that sufficient Irish be heard by other speeches. If you can come and name your

---

[102] . Jordan Anthony J. *Boer War to Easter Rising The Writings of John MacBrde*, Westport 2006. pp. 11-83.

subject, and the most suitable Friday between this and Easter? If Friday does not suit we could perhaps arrange another evening.

Yours sincerely
PH Pearse".

The letter, apart from the signature was typed. A postscript, in poor handwriting at the bottom of the page added;
"P.S. What the boys would really like is an account of your experience in the South African War"[103].

The Easter Rebellion at Dublin in 1916 took most people by surprise. Only a small select group of conspirators knew what was planned. They determined that England's difficulty would again be Ireland's opportunity. Small groups of men and women took over key buildings on Easter Monday. In London the War Office issued orders to General Maxwell, which read; *"The Army Council under powers conferred on them by Regulation 62 , Defense of The Realm Regulations , hereby appoint Lieutenant-General Sir J. Maxwell K.C.B. Commander in Chief of the forces in Ireland , to be a competent military authority under these regulations ; with power to delegate , either unconditionally or subject to such conditions as he may think fit , all or any of his powers under these regulations to any officer qualified to be appointed a Competent Military Authority".* 28/4/1916.

Two days later an Army Communique read; *"One of the Principal Rebel Leaders, P.H.Pearse, is known to be inside the cordon suffering from a fractured thigh.The woman known as Countess Markievcz has also been seen inside. Another Leader, James Connolly is reported killed. Arrangements are being made to intern in England all Sinn Feiners captured or surrendered, who are not dealt with here ".*

---

[103] . Manuscript 26,755 NLI.

The city center had been devastated and hundreds were killed. Martial law was introduced and thousands of Nationalists interned. The news from Dublin to the outside world was very sparse as most of the newspapers did not publish and military censorship was imposed. Rumor spread that it was the start of a German or a Socialist coup. Opinion on it was mixed in the confusion. The battles lasted all week long until the Rebels surrendered on the Saturday. The order to surrender came in a hand written message from Pearse in the General Post Office. It read;

"In order to prevent the slaughter of unarmed people and in the hope of saving the lives of our followers, the Members of the Provisional Government present at Headquarters agreed last night to an unconditional surrender , and Commandants or Commanding Officers of Districts will order their men to lay down their arms or disband "
P.H. Pearse 30th April 1916.

John MacBride had met Commandant Thomas MacDonagh on Easter Monday morning who invited him to accompany his troops to take over Jacob's Biscuit factory. MacBride did so and due to his military experience in South Africa became the effective commander at Jacobs. After Patrick Pearse issued the order to surrender, Peadar Kearney discussed leaving before the surrender became effective with Major MacBride. MacBride replied, *"Liberty is a priceless thing and any of you that sees a chance, take it. I'd do so myself, but my liberty days are over. Good luck boys. Many of you may live to fight some other day. Take my advice and never allow yourself to be cooped up inside the walls of a building again"*[104]. The Cumann na mBan women did not wish to leave. MacBride spoke to the Abbey Theatre actress Maire ni Shiubhlaigh saying *"it would be better for you to go"*. He asked her to pass on a message to her neighbor, Clara Allan of Glenageary, the woman he loved: *"Tell them that we had a good week of it"*. Nic Shiubhlaigh wrote of MacBride, *"he fulfilled all the expectations as a soldier of courage and resource, a gentleman, quiet, witty, always unruffled. Without exception, the Volunteers in the building admired and respected him"*[105].

---

[104] . Peadar O'Cearnaigh Story, as recorded by his nephew Seamus de Burca. Trinity College Archves.
[105] . Maire Nic Shiublaigh The Splendid Years

Maud was in Normandy with her family that Easter, when the news broke that there was trouble in Dublin. She was desperate to find out what was happening.Willie was in London promising to send Maud the papers as soon as they were to hand again. On the Thursday after the Rising finished a military communique was published. It read;
"Three *signatories of the notice proclaiming the Irish Republic P.H.Pearse, T. Mac Donagh and T. Clarke have been tried by Field General court martial and sentenced to death.*
The sentence having been duly confirmed, the three above mentioned men were shot this morning. The trial of further prisoners is proceeding".

Maud was thunderstruck. She had met and liked the three dead men. News quickly followed that her own husband was being held and would soon face trial. James Connolly, Constance Markievcz, Helena Moloney were also to be court martialled. Arthur Griffith and Joseph MacBride and many more of her friends were interned.

Two days later another communique was published saying four more executions had taken place. A day later Maud read that John MacBride had been executed too. He had not been part of the inner conspiracy but was in the city early to meet his brother Dr. Anthony who was coming to Dublin to be married on the Wednesday. John was to be Best Man. He met Thomas MacDonagh and a party of armed volunteers; discovering what was going on he offered his services and was accepted. Due to his experience in the Boar War MacDonagh made him Vice Commandant at Jacob's Factory. He proved a very successful leader during the week as several of the survivors have attested. The British couldn't believe their luck in capturing their Boer War enemy under arms. General Maxwell had seen service in the Transvaal and he had been spared from execution there at a critical stage. MacBride faced his executioners without a blindfold, saying he was used to facing English guns. The sole witness he called at his court-martial was Clara Allan, the lady he loved, who later converted to Catholicism to be closer to MacBride. The Allans hid MacBride's papers which were only transferred to the National Library of Ireland in the 1970's, under the name of *"The Fred Allan Papers"*. These papers which contained the submissions to the Parisian Divorce Court from both parties in 1905 formed the basis for my 2000 book, *The Yeats Gonne MacBride Triangle*.

With the newspaper sent by Willie still in her hands and without any emotion, Maud told Iseult *"MacBride has been shot "*. Neither shed any tears. She told her son that his father had given his life for the sake of Ireland and though he was not so kind to them, he was now a man of honor. *"We can all be proud to have the name of MacBride forever"* she said, *"He is a hero. Those who die for Ireland are sacred. They enter Eternity by the great door of Sacrifice Atone for all - "*. Maud told Yeats that Ireland was a sadder but a prouder place now. *"It has some dignity restored. I will come to London as soon as possible when I get a passport"*[106] she wrote. Yeats too couldn't believe how he was so affected by news of the events.

The executions continued in Dublin. Four days later, four more men were shot. After another interval of four days the last two executions occurred. Sean MacDiarmada and the wounded James Connolly, propped up in a chair were shot. Helena Moloney was held in Kilmainham jail. Two leaders of the Rising escaped execution, Eamon De Valera because he was an American citizen and Constance Markievcz, because she was a woman. Their death sentences were commuted to life imprisonment. Maud, though marooned in France had not even to consider her attitude to the Rising. It had been a National necessity. It was in the long tradition of Irish Risings against the English occupiers. The fact that there was so much destruction and loss of life among people she knew well numbed her at first. But later she felt happy for them. They had been faithful. They had claimed their place among the lists of Irish heroes. She was proud of them and eager to return to Dublin to continue the struggle.

For Willie it was not so easy. He was basically a literary man drawn into Republicanism by the desire to be with Maud. But he was a Nationalist, though not a physical force one. Yet he too, as he told

---

[106] . *Gonne-Yeats Letters* p. 375.

139

Maud was excited by the nobility of it all. He too saw it as a gesture by some idealists and other hardnosed men, to rouse the Irish people to throw off the shackles of British Imperialism. He was well aware of the poetic involvement in the Rising.

Willie was to produce his first poem on the Rising very shortly. He called it "*Easter 1916* ". He began it by saying how he was on nodding acquaintance with many of the participants; ordinary people they seemed with ordinary jobs. He did not take their republicanism seriously. But they suddenly have created a shocking situation which is also a beautiful one. The '*ignorant woman*' he mentions is Countess Markievcz, who gave up an easy life. '*This other his helper and friend* ' is the poet Thomas MacDonagh, who taught in Pearse's school, St. Enda's. '*This other man I had dreamed a drunken, vainglorious lout*' is Willie's backhanded tribute to Major John Mac Bride. This highlighting of her estranged husband infuriated Maud. She thought poorly of Willie's poem and told him it did not do justice to its subject either. She emphasized to Willie that her husband had atoned for anything he had done against her. By his death she could pray for him and even to him! At the end of the poem Willie does pose the question that many asked; '*was their sacrifice needless, may be England would have kept her promise and given Ireland her freedom?* Nevertheless it does not lessen one whit the beauty they were nursemaids to. They have changed everything. He wrote it out in a verse.

EASTER 1916

I have met them at close of day
Coming with vivid faces
From counter or desk among grey
Eighteenth-century houses.
I have passed with a nod of the head
 Or polite meaningless words,
 Or have lingered awhile and said

Polite meaningless words,
And thought before I had done
Of a mocking tale or a gibe
To please a companion
Around the fire at the club,
Being certain that they and I
But lived where motley is worn:
All changed, changed utterly:
A terrible beauty is born.

That woman's days were spent
In ignorant good-will,
Her nights in argument
Until her voice grew shrill.
What voice more sweet than hers
When, young and beautiful,
She rode to harriers?
This man had kept a school
And rode our winged horse;
This other his helper and friend
Was coming into his force;
He might have won fame in the end,
So sensitive his nature seemed,
So daring and sweet his thought.
This other man I had dreamed
A drunken, vainglorious lout.
He had done most bitter wrong
To some who are near my heart,
Yet I number him in the song;
He, too, has resigned his part
In the casual comedy;
He, too, has been changed in his turn,
Transformed utterly:
A terrible beauty is born...

When Willie sent the poem to Maud in November, she was not impressed writing to him in no uncertain terms;

My dear Willie,

> *No I don't like your poem, it isn't worthy of you & above all it isn't worthy of the subject-*
> *Sacrifice has never yet turned a heart to stone though it has immortalized many & through it alone can mankind can rise to God...But you could never say that MacDonagh Pearse and Connolly were sterile faced minds, each served Ireland, which was their share of the world, the part they were in contact with, with varied faculties and vivid energy! Those three were men of genius...*
> *As for my husband he has entered Eternity by the great door of sacrifice which Christ opened & has therefore atoned for all so that praying for him I can also ask for his prayers, & 'A Terrible beauty is born'*
> *There are beautiful lines in your poem, as there are in all you write but it is not a great WHOLE, a living thing which our race would treasure & repeat, such as a poet like you might have given to your nation & which would have avenged our material failure by its spiritual beauty-*
> *You will be angry perhaps that I write so frankly what I feel, but I am always frank with my friends & though our ideals are wide apart we are still friends[107].*

When Willie saw that Maud was upset about his first poem on the Rising he felt he should proceed to write about another participant whom they both knew very well. This man was Jim Connolly who in some ways was the most tragic figure of the Rising. He was looking for a Socialist Republic first and foremost. Yet he felt he had to join in when the moment came and hope that his faith and sacrifice would also bear fruit. Willie knew that Maud admired Connolly intensely and would miss him as an activist, always ready for the most daring or humdrum task. He titled his poem "*The Rose Tree*".

He compared Ireland to a Rose Tree which is not blooming because of too much talking and contact with England. Connolly says the

---

[107]. Gonne-Yeats Leters p. 384.

tree needs sustenance. Pearse replies that only their blood will give life to the tree.

The Rose Tree

O words are lightly spoken
Said Pearse to Connolly,
Maybe a breath of politic words
Has withered our Rose Tree;
Or maybe but a wind that blows
Across the bitter sea'.

It needs to be but watered
James Connolly replied
To make the green come out again
And spread on every side,
And shake the blossom from the bud
To be the garden's pride.

But where can we draw water
Said Pearse to Connolly,
'When all the wells are parched away?
O plain as plain can be
There's nothing but our own red blood
Can make a right Rose Tree'.

Maud was very pleased with *"The Rose Tree"* and congratulated Willie. She felt he was reading the mood of Nationalism Ireland correctly. She had maintained contact with her old friend John Daly of Limerick, whose family remained at the center of Irish republicanism. His sister Kathleen had married Tom Clarke in New York with John MacBride as Best Man. His nephew Edward Daly was another of the sixteen executed. Sean Mac Diarmada who was partially crippled with poliomyelitis and executed last, with Jim Connolly had been friendly with one of the Daly girls and knew the family intimately. MacDiarmada wrote to John Daly, then an old man and close to death the night before his execution. Daly sent the letter on to Maud suggesting that Yeats might be interested in seeing. It read;

Kilmainham Prison
II/5/1/I6
My Dear Daly,
Just a wee note to bid you Goodbye. I expect in a few hours to join Tom and the other heroes in a better world. I have been sentenced to a soldier's death-- to be shot tomorrow morning. I have nothing to say about this only I look on it as part of the day's work. We die that the Irish nation may live. Our blood will be baptism and reinvigorate the old land. Knowing this it is superfluous to say how ' happy ' I feel. I know now what I have always felt that the Irish nation can never die. Let present day place hunters condemn our action as they will, posterity will judge us a right from the effects of our action.
I know I will meet you soon. Until then goodbye. God guard you and protect you and all in number 15.You have had a sore trial but I know quite well that Mrs. Daly and all the girls feel proud in spite of a little temporary and natural grief that her son and the girls their brother as well as Tom are included in the list of honors. Kindly remember me to Mrs. Clarke and tell her I am the same Sean that she always knew.
God bless you all
Sean MacDiarmada ".

Willie read MacDiarmada's letter in Maud's house in Normandy. He was deeply moved and did not speak for some time. Maud did not interrupt but remained in silence with him. His third poem about the Rising had a harder, more militant ring about it. He says that after Easter Week people had varied views about the Rising. But the execution of the Sixteen changed all that. Their presence would not go away. Some said they should wait until the World War ended before pursuing matters. But that could not be when the old patriots found new comrades.

SIXTEEN DEAD MEN

O but we talked at large before
The sixteen men were shot,
But who can talk of give and take,
What should be and what not
While those dead men are loitering there
To stir the boiling pot?

You say that we should still the land
Till Germany's overcome;
But who is there to argue that
Now Pearse is deaf and dumb?
And is their logic to outweigh
MacDonagh's bony thumb?

How could you dream they'd listen
That have an ear alone
For those new comrades they have found,
Lord Edward and Wolfe Tone,
Or meddle with our give and take
That converse bone to bone?

Maud was staying in the South of France near Lourdes in 1917 as wounded French soldiers from the front were brought locally to recover. She wrote *"The Mayor of Argeles came up one day to our village and asked any women who knew anything about nursing to come and nurse the wounded as there were not enough trained nurses. The municipal hospital was so crowded that they converted the Casino into a hospital, but they had no nurses for it. I volunteered although I was not trained, but I had some experience. From that on people were not allowed to travel without passports. I could not leave my children alone in a war-invaded country as the Germans were advancing very rapidly. So I came down and took rooms in a tiny house in Argeles where I was nursing. Helena Molony eventually succeeded in getting back to Dublin. The trains were arriving with the wounded and when Helena had left, Iseult began to nurse also. Sean ingratiated himself with the wounded soldiers by acting as a sort of page boy bringing messages, etc. It was said that the French lost 50% of their wounded for the lack of trained nurses[108].*

This experience of the casualties of war turned her towards pacifism.

When she returned to Paris she again volunteered to assist the wounded soldiers. She was still refused a passport. So she decided to send Iseult to London to join with Yeats in trying to get permission for her to travel. Iseult was a French citizen and so was free to travel. She made the Channel crossing safely and reported to Willie that her mother was getting more annoyed that she was not able to travel herself. Iseult also told Willie that Maud wanted him to organize legal help for Helena Moloney and other members of her "*Daughters of Erin* " who were in jail. Then Maud wanted Willie to escort Iseult back to Normandy. Iseult was aged twenty two and a more seductive woman than her mother. She had a very tender, almost plaintiff look about her, which with her pouting lips made her look a most vulnerable and ethereally pale creature.Willie, then aged fifty couldn't believe he had not been struck by her beauty before. Then he realized this was the first time he had met her without her mother being around. He took great pleasure in showing her off too many of his friends who were equally impressed. He wrote a short poem for her comparing her to her own mother who had broken his heart.

TO A YOUNG GIRL

My dear, my dear, I know
More than another
What makes your heart beat so;
Not even your own mother
Can know it as I know,
Who broke my heart for her
When the wild thought,

---

[108] . Bureau of Military History Statement 1949.

That she denies
And has forgotten.
Set all her blood astir
And glittered in her eyes.

Chapter 16.

BROKEN DREAMS

Willie spent the summer months at *Les Mouettes* in Normandy with Maud and her family. He was writing part of his autobiography and reading. Iseult acted as his secretary almost out of habit. He again asked Maud to marry him and again she refused. Maud could see that he then became infatuated with Iseult. He asked Maud's permission to propose to Iseult, who prevaricated. Willie had wrtten to Lady Gregory, *"Iseult and I take long walks, and are as we were last year affectionate and intimate and she shows many little signs of affection"*.

Iseult

Willie left Normandy for London and Maud and family returned to Paris. It was winter. The slaughter of younger and younger men continued on the War front. Maud and Iseult became nurses ministering to the wounded. The horror of the results of war demonstrated to Maud that there was no dignity in suffering and that violence should not be countenanced. Henceforth she would dedicate her life to prisoners and the poor.

Quite suddenly Maud's passport arrived and she was free to travel. Full of excitement they packed. The day before they were due to travel the British War Office announced that Madame MacBride wouldn't be allowed to travel on to Ireland. Maud rained fury towards British politicians. She sought support from the Irish Parliamentary Party. Willie wrote to say that she might get a passport for Ireland but first she would have to renounce political activity. It was a long cold and hungry winter in Paris. In Ireland some of those arrested were released, but not Joseph MacBride who was very ill.

In early summer Maud received a First Anniversary Memorial Card from Mrs. MacBride in Wesport commemorating Major John MacBride.It read;

John MacBride   Executed 5/51916
First Anniversary I dCuimhne Ar
* Sheaghan Mac Giolla Brighide Major John MacBride*
Vice Commandant Irish Republican Army; Major in the Army of the South African Republic , Organizer of the Transvaal Irish Brigade.
Who died for Ireland 5th May 1916
Go ndeanfhaidh Dia Trocaire Ara Anam[109] .

Sinn Fein was now the main party of Nationalism in Ireland and it gradually began to win some crucial bye-elections.The spirit generated by the 1916 Rising was becoming very clear. The Irish Parliamentary Party and their goal of Home Rule was outdated. A separate Parliament completely independent from Westminster was now the aim. Arthur Griffith's dream was now the policy.

Maud decided that she would travel on to Ireland from London. She wanted her son to start school in Ireland that autumn. Willie decided that when Iseult eventually refused his proposal, he would marry a London friend, Georgie Hyde-Lees., At Southampton Docks Maud and Iseult had to undergo the indignity of being physically searched. Maud was served with an order under the *Defense of the Realm Act* confining her to Britain.Willie felt responsible for them still despite his rejections. He got a job for Iseult as a Librarian. He arranged for his friend, Ezra Pound to teach young Seaghan. Maud decided to return to Art school. It was a time of great emotional strain for Willie. He commemorated this time with his *"Broken Dreams"* poem.

BROKEN DREAMS

---

[109] . Jordan Anthony J. *Willie Yeats and the Gonne MacBrides*, Westport 1997. p. 149.

There is grey in your hair.
Young men no longer suddenly catch their breath
When you are passing;
But maybe some old gaffer 'nutters a blessing
Because it was your prayer
Recovered him upon the bed of death.
Or your sole sake—that all heart's ache have known,
And given to others all heart's ache,
From meagre girlhood's putting on
Burdensome beauty for your sake
Heaven has put away the stroke of her doom
So great was her portion in that peace you make
By merely walking in a room...

This point marked the end of Willie's youthful endeavors. He was about to face up to reality. The next month he got married. The public was fascinated to discover Maud's reaction. But there was none. She never wanted him as a husband, only as a friend and confidant. She believed he would still remain that, with his wife as young as Iseult. Remarkably George and Iseult became very close friends and Iseult often stayed with the newlyweds. For the first time Willie had someone who really loved him. She turned out to be a perfect wife. He had met her through their mutual interest in spiritualism. Shortly after this Willie took George to live in an old damp tower he had bought at Coole, not far from where Lady Gregory lived in Ireland. Maud and her family moved into his vacated apartment at Woburn Buildings London, where she and Willie had spent so much time.

Maud continued to wage her campaign for permission to travel on to Ireland. She cultivated the friendship of Charlotte Despard, a Socialist and feminist, whose brother was Lord French, the Viceroy designated to Ireland. He had been in command of the British forces at the battle of Ypres. Maud spoke at Sylvia Pankhurst's Suffragette Party about Irish freedom. She criticized the Government for refusing a widow and her son permission to visit MacBride's grave. She tried to get permission to have his body exhumed from the common grave where those executed were buried, but to no avail. One small piece of good news for her was the passing of the Representation of the People Act in December 1917, giving the vote to women over thirty.

Maud soon got fed up waiting and decided that direct action was called for if she was to return to Ireland. Disguising herself and her son, they boarded a train in London, travelled to Holyhead and boarded the ferry for Kingstown. She had alerted a friend and Helena Moloney met her at the harbour. At first Maud kept a low profile in Dublin. But her nature got the better of her and gradually she became involved with her usual forms of agitation over social conditions and nationalism. She came to the notice of the police, but they did not interfere. She now called herself Maud Gonne MacBride. This annoyed many people who thought it hypocritical and typical of her opportunism. But she wanted to clearly establish her son's identity in the public domain and couldn't care less what people said. Her son now also became known as Sean rather than Seaghan or Jean. He joined the Fianna, a junior branch of the Irish Republican Army connected to Sinn Fein and set up by Constance Marckievcz.

Lady Gregory's son Robert was killed in the War in France. The day after his death a distraught Lady Gregory wrote to Yeats: *'Robert has been killed in action. It is very hard to bear. If you feel like it sometime, write something down that we may keep. You understood him better than many.'* Two poems were written that summer by Yeats, *In Memory of Major Robert Gregory* and the better known *An Irish Airman Foresees His Death,* which has come to epitomize the Great War airman's romantic desire to live for the moment, when issues of life and death are in such precarious balance. Maud travelled to Coole Park to offer her sympathies in person. She also visited Willie and his wife in their Tower which she found rather dreary. Willie was extremely happy with George.

The death of Robert Gregory had a profound effect on Yeats. He felt that he could understand the strange predicament of many of the Anglo-Irish to the War which could not be understood in London. They were British, yet they were also Irish, and their lives were based locally. The War seemed so futile especially for Robert Gregory. Yeats visualizes Robert as expecting to die in the war. He has no hatred for those he was fighting. He did not love the British. He comes from rural Ireland where the outcome of the war will have no effect on the lives of the people. He did not have to join the fighting forces. There was no pressure on him. But the excitement of it all claimed him. His life seemed to be monotonous, so why shouldn't he put it all at risk amoung the clouds?

AN IRISH AIRMAN FORESEES HIS DEATH

I know that I shall meet my fate
Somewhere among the clouds above;
Those that I fight I do not hate,
Those that I guard I do not love;
My country is Kiltartan Cross,
My countrymen Kiltartan's poor,
No likely end could bring them loss
Or leave them happier than before.
Nor law nor duty bade me fight,
No public men, nor cheering crowds,
A lonely impulse of delight
Drove to this tumult in the clouds;
I balanced all, brought all to mind,
The years to come seemed waste of breath,
A waste of breath the years behind
In balance with this life, this death.

On the Continent the War was going badly for the Allies. Von Ludendorff had advanced to within forty miles of Paris, and captured 80,000 men. It looked like he would soon reach the Channel itself. The Government introduced Conscription. This was opposed in Ireland. Lord French, the new Viceroy in Ireland discovered a ' *German Plot*' and arrested 73 leadings activists and interned them without trial. Arthur Griffith, Constance Marckievcz and Eamon DeValera were among those. Two days later Tom Clarke's widow, Kathleen, and John MacBride's widow were also interned. As Maud was being taken away in the police van, she could see her fourteen old son run alongside. Maud, Kathleen and Constance shared a landing in Hollaway Prison in London. They had left six children behind them in Ireland.

Maud spent five and a half shocking months in jail. Unlike Constance, she was not tough, physically or mentally for incarceration. Her health deteriorated rapidly. There was no just reason for her to be interned. She considered applying for a concessionary release at a low ebb, but Maud was quickly brought into line by Constance saying, "*This would be totally against the traditions of political prisoners. You would become a pariah in republican circles forever. I would never have anything to do with you again. Your name would be disgraced. You just cannot do it. I will not allow it* ".The only concession Maud was allowed was to have her pet canary could stay in the prison with her. She began to spend most of her prison days talking to it. Yeats and other friends tried in vain to have her released.

One day Maud was called to the Prison Governor's office. She had to '*request*' permission of Constance to go. There the Governor told her he had a letter from the Home Office which he was to read to her. Maud felt sure it was to be her unconditional release. *"You are requested to inform the prisoner that a Lucien Millevoye has died in Paris*", the man behind the desk read as Maud stood before him," *that is all. You may return to your cell*"[110]. Back in her cell she had to tell Constance the news, not that she would understood its significance. Maud showed no outward sign of grief but repeatedly said the governor's sentence over and over to the canary, "*You are requested to inform the prisoner that a Lucien Millevoye has died in Paris* ". His daughter Iseult wrote to her mother that she had read the heart-breaking news in the papers.

---

[110] . Ward Margaret, *Maud Gonne Ireland's Joan of Arc*, Pandora 1990. p. 119.

Some week's later even worse news was brought to Maud. Her sister, Kathleen had been in a sanatorium in France, ever since her eldest son had been killed in the War there. Now she too died. It was the blackest moment for Maud since her baby had died all those years ago. Iseult feared for her mother's life. Yeats feared for her sanity. He redoubled his efforts to have her released.

After five months an outside doctor was eventually allowed in to the prison to examine Maud. The doctor found that she had tuberculosis. With this information her friends exerted more pressure on the authorities. Yeats asked "*do they want to make a martyr of her too?*" Finally she was released, but much to her indignation, into Iseult's custody. Sean came to London and they all lived at Woburn Buildings again. Willie Yeats rented their Dublin house while they occupied his.

The end of the War brought relief to all. But Maud wondered why Ireland was not included by President Wilson when he spoke of freedom for small nations at the Peace Conference. 49,000 Irish had died in the War, several receiving Victoria Crosses. A General Election was called. LLoyd George retracted on the 1914 Home Rule Bill for Ireland. "*Ulster should not be coerced*" he told the House of Commons. Sinn Fein fought the Election on the platform that if elected they would set up a Parliament in Dublin. Many of Maud's friends and colleagues, some still in jail, were Sinn Fein candidates. They won 73 seats to 6 for the Irish Parliamentary Party. The Unionists won 26 seats. Maud fretted in London. Once more she was away from the action in Ireland. She was confined to Britain and faced jail if she returned to Ireland.

But finally Maud could not bear being away. She decided to return illegally, taking Iseult and Sean with her. The boat from Holyhead moved gingerly through the narrow gap of Kingstown's harbor wall. It was six o'clock in the morning. Within a half an hour Maud and her two children were getting into a carriage on the sea front. Maud had decided it would be too risky informing anybody she was returning. As the horse trotted along the Monkstown Road towards

Blackrock and the city, the three passengers were very tired and cold. The carriage stopped outside number 73 St. Stephen's Green which was owned by Maud but occupied by Willie and his wife. The driver climbed down from his seat and knocked on the door. Eventually a lady appeared and was asked was Mr Yeats at home. The servant closed the door and after about ten minutes Mr Yeats appeared dressed in a huge overcoat and nightcap. He was not pleased to see Maud and a row developed between them. His wife was ill and he knew that Maud had travelled to Ireland illegally exposing him as an accessory if he let her in. Maud turned on her heel and walked back to the carriage and gave instructions to drive to Helena Moloney's house[111].

News of this event soon became public knowledge within the nationalist community. The militant Cumann na mBan made serious charges against Yeats for conspiring with the enemy in exposing Maud to danger of being arrested. This incident was without doubt another turning point in their relationship.

Willie and Maud knew each other too well and too long to allow ill feeling to remain. Very soon they patched up their unfortunate quarrel. They resumed their unique relationship, though like them, it was changing too. Willie's hair was now silver and his shortsightedness was notorious. He was soon to produce a new version of "Cathleen Ni Houlihan" at the Abbey Theatre. Maud and Iseult attended the first night, thereby publicly announcing that any enmity between them was at an end. Lady Gregory played the leading part, originally written for and played by Maud. Lady Gregory was now old and Maud herself though her walk was still regal, was going grey.

Maud's life was now in Ireland. She recovered her house at St. Stephen's Green from Yeats. It became a meeting place for various people, ardent socialists to militant republicans, suffragettes and socialites. Willie Yeats and his literary circle were regular friends. But Maud had been changed by her experiences. Violence had no aura for her now. She hated its necessity and couldn't participate.

---

[111]. Jordan, WB Yeats op. cit. p. 111.

Prison became a great evil for her and prisoners a cause for life. She didn't join Sinn Fein. She made no attempt to become an insider in the National Movement. She remained an outsider, a protester free to take up any cause. Politics and constitutional politics still remained anathema,

The new Irish Parliament meeting in Dublin was declared illegal. The British Government was not sure how to handle the ensuing chaos. The I.R.A.began to ambush security forces starting a guerilla war. The Government introduced Special Forces called *Black and Tans* into the country. They terrorized the people and the Dirty War of Reprisals began. Atrocities became common place. Many political prisoners were held in terrible conditions. Maud became heavily involved on their behalf. Charlotte Despard came to stay with Maud and help with the conditions around the country. She was an embarrassment to the authorities as Lord French's sister, but a safe escort for Maud among the *Black and Tans*.

A women's' committee organised a lobby of the U.S.A. Congress. An American Committee for relief in Ireland won official approval. One million pounds became available for relief in Ireland. *The White Cross* was set up in Dublin to co-ordinate the relief. Maud and Kathleen Clarke were on the Committee. The Sinn Fein Government were all on the run and unavailable. Children were fed, allowances paid, businesses supported, homes built, all via Local Public Boards. These had plumped for Sinn Fein and had their funds stopped by the British. Arthur Griffith was acting President of Ireland when Maud wrote, reporting the conditions in the country to him. Sylvia Pankhurst came to visit Maud and support the cause.

Unknown to Maud her son was heavily involved in the war. He was reading Law at University but put it aside to take up arms. One night a car he was driving was stopped. Constance Markievcz and an official from the French Government were his passengers. All were arrested. Sean was released in a few days but Constance was sentenced to two years. Shortly after this when Sean was cleaning his rifle at home in Stephens Green, the gun went off accidentally.

Then his mother knew for sure that he was involved. She feared for him but couldn't do much else.

On one Sunday morning 14 British undercover agents were assassinated in Dublin. That same afternoon the army raided Croke Park where a Gaelic football match was in progress. They shot dead 12 and wounded 60. A young Galway boy was arrested and charged with complicity in the mornings events. He was sentenced to death. His mother came to Dublin and stayed with Maud. The two women held a vigil outside Mountjoy as the boy was hanged within. Forty Irish hunger strikers were set free from Wormwood Scrubs to avoid making martyrs of them. Thirty abandoned police stations in Co. Cork were burned. There was mounting pressure from the International Community for the Government to settle the Irish problem by peaceful means. A ceasefire was negotiated. Lloyd George spoke with De Valera. Discussions were to take place in London.

In the meantime Maud had been having domestic difficulties. Iseult had eloped with a Northerner, eight years her junior, named Francis Stuart. Maud panicked and determined scandal would not be revisited on the family. She insisted the couple marry, after Francis became a Catholic first. Stuart was a poet and Yeats was one of his heroes. The flippancy which his wife and mother-in law displayed to Yeats did not endear them to him; it made him furious. As relations between Stuart and the two women worsened they called in Willie himself to try to ease the hostility.

As soon as the truce between the two armies was signed Maud took the whole family including Stuart to Bavaria for a holiday. The poor rate of exchange for the Mark was making made other currencies very valuable. The Irish were welcome visitors to the land of Wagner. Sean was first to return home. Unknown to Maud he had been buying guns which he hid in a recess cut into books, and posted back to a safe address in Dublin. Maud returned later leaving Iseult and Francis behind her.

During the Anglo-Irish Truce only Members elected to the Parliament were released. A few women prisoners escaped from Mountjoy. Maud gave a safe house to one of them until the search ended. Constance Markievcz visited during the prisoners stay. The Sinn Fein delegation left for the Treaty negotiations in London without their leader De Valera, who refused to travel. Sean McBride though only 17, travelled with the delegation as Aide-de-Camp to Michael Collins the Minister for Finance. Arthur Griffith, a friend of Maud's for many years, was the delegation leader. For two months the talks dragged on. Maud worried for the safety of Sean and all the delegation in London. Finally under threat by Lloyd George of *"Terrible War within three days"*, The Articles of Agreement or Treaty were signed.

Chapter 17

SEAN *TURNS* HIS MOTHER

Sean or Seaghan as he was called in his childhood in Paris, whose custody had been the main cause of the bitterness of his mother's divorce case from his father, gradually became the main man in her life, as her radicalism caused a long-term silence with Yeats. She was to follow Sean's star for the rest of her life. As Nancy Cardozo writes: *"Many of Maud's ideals, her compassion for human suffering, her belief in individual liberty, were Sean's. Even her feminist views had been transmitted to her son. He had grown up among women of an unusually independent nature"[112]*

Sean MacBride had spent his most formative years in an almost exclusively female environment. This left a mark on him for all of his life as he found it easier to establish close personal and working relationships with women, who were usually attracted to him[113]+ [114].When he was four he was sent to school at the Jesuit College, St. Louis de Gonzaga, on Rue Franklin in Paris. He was not a very healthy boy enduring many childhood illnesses. He made his first Holy Communion in 1911, where his name on the group souvenir was Jean Gonne. The next month he and his mother were received in a private audience by Pope Pius X. In 1913 he was confirmed by Cardinal Amette, Archbishop of Paris. In the spring of 1914 Maud brought him to Dublin where he met Patrick Pearse, headmaster of St Enda's School, where his mother intended he would attend school in the event of the family moving to live in Ireland. Willie Yeats, who was a frequent visitor to their home, described Sean thus: *The little boy is now quite tall and is going to be very clever and to my amusement has begun to criticize his mother's politics. He has a confident and analytic mind and is more like a boy of seventeen than thirteen".*

---

[112] .Cardozo Nancy, *Maud Gonne*, Gollancz 1989 p. 398.
[113] . Jordan Anthony J. *Sean A Biography of Sean MacBride*, Blackwatwer Press 1993, pp. 161-162.

Sean spoke of how his school handled news of the execution of his father in 1916, saying: *"I was at school in Paris. I must say I have had tremendous affection for the Jesuits for the way they handled the situation. They were very good because at that time France was fighting Germany, with Britain as an ally. Our Rising was against the British. The Germans were quite close to Paris at the time and you could hear the artillery. They had a commemoration day every week for the parents of those boys who had been killed and on this day the Director of the school came out and made a most moving speech, explaining that France was at war, in order to protect the liberty of small nations and to ensure that justice was done in the world. He explained that while my father was not fighting on the same side as the French he was fighting for the freedom of a small nation, Ireland, and they all had tremendous sympathy for what the Irish people were trying to do ... It was a great way of smoothing things out in the school; as well, all the other boys understood[115].*

On his coming to live permanently in Dublin Sean quickly began to associate himself with the republican militants. Due to his name and ancestry he was treated differently to other activists. His French accent gave him an added sense of mystery. Tod Andrews explains: *"He was brought up in situations where he only met the important people in the Independence movement. He behaved from boyhood as if he was one of them. He was accepted as such by everyone he met. A tall man, with thin nondescript hair, his features were finely wrought, but his hollow cheeks and deep set haunted eyes gave him something of the appearance of a character in a Gothic novel. He spoke in a peculiarly soothing manner. He was extremely brave and had an aristocratic indifference to money. On the question of Separation MacBride never lost the Fenian faith"[116].*

Sean himself wrote in 1948 to Lord Jowett, Chancellor in Clement Attlee's 1945-1951 Labor Government.

---

[115]. RTe Interview *Soundings* 1979
[116]. Andrews C.S. *Man of No Property* Mercier 1982. p.35.

When I was very young my father was executed for his part in the 1916 rising. My mother was in jail and on hunger strike several times. I was in school in France but I arrived here at the age of 14 and I promptly found myself in jail. From that time until 1921 I was in jail or 'on the run' continuously up to the Treaty and during the Civil War...Two successive governments, Mr. Cosgrave's and Mr. deValera continually made, I believe, bone fide attempts to end 'continuous incipient civil wars'. These attempts failed...Coercion Acts, internment, hunger strikes, Military Courts, Executions, suppression, censorship, hunger strikes...For over ten years I remained on the sideline watching the same conflict going on, coming into contact with it only in my professional capacity[117].

Sean was in London as an *aide* in 1921 for the Anglo-Irish Treaty negotiations. He stayed with the army wing of the Irish delegation to the Treaty Talks at Cadogan Square, where Michael Collins also lodged, rather than at Hans Place where the politicians lodged. Sean found *"a tremendous dichotomy between the two houses"*. He spent most of his time *"running dispatches from London to Dublin. Many of these I delivered directly to de Valera or to Kathleen O'Connell, who was his private secretary"*[118] Eventually the Irish Delegation under threat of *"immediate and terrible war "*"signed a Treaty and brought it back to the Government and Dail for ratification.

During the resulting Dail Debates to ratify the Treaty, the Cabinet and Dail split down the middle. The bitterest charges were made. Maud felt that to let six counties of Ulster secede from its own Parliament and for the 26 counties to have its own Parliament, but within the Dominion of Britain, was not what was sought. But she also knew many people were satisfied with it as a start. Yeats feared the country would be destroyed by Civil War. The Dail voted to accept the Treaty by 64 votes to 57. Griffith was elected President of Dail Eireann with de Valera leading the Opposition. All the elected women opposed to the Treaty. There was no Irish Republic only an Irish Free State.   Sean McBride wrote, *"I was*

---

[117] . MacBride to Lord Jowitt 4 October 1948 No. 154. DFA.
[118] . MacBride Sean, That Day's Struggle p. 44-45.

completely opposed to it ...and offered my services to deValera[119]. Sean tried unsuccessfully to get his mother to oppose it publicly, writing, *"I also had disagreements at home. Mother was at that time very much in favour of the Treaty. I could well understand her point of view. Most of her lifetime, the struggle had been largely for Home Rule. To Mother this looked like a tremendous step forward...I felt that we should have gone further. So Mother and I fell out over this"*[120].

For Maud it meant the end of bloodletting. Griffith appointed her as an official delegate to the *Irish Race Convention* in Paris. Willie Yeats, Doughlas Hyde and Constance Markievcz also attended. But though it was mainly a cultural occasion the split over the Treaty carried through there. But Maud and Constance, despite their political differences, maintained their friendship. DeValera attended the Convention and Sean MacBride, then living in Paris acted as his 'aide de com'. Sean T. O'Kelly was running the Irish embassy and living in the biggest and most expensive hotel in Paris. MacBride comments, *"Sean T. was inclined to be rather lavish"*[121].

The British army were moving out of the 26 counties and handing over to the new Free State Army. But those opposed to the Treaty especially part of the I.R.A. began to take over Army and Government installations as well. The new State was having great difficulty assuming its responsibilities with such irregular activities spreading throughout the country. The most blatant place this had occurred was in the Four Courts Complex in Dublin. Some militant Republicans including Sean McBride and his wife to be Catalina Bulfin defied the new Government's Authority and fortified the place. The British issued an ultimatum to the new Government. It must assert its control by taking the Four Courts or else the Treaty was abrogated.

In Paris Maud was working for Desmond Fitzgerald, Minister for Publicity. It was vital that the world hear of the difficulties the new

---

[119] .MacBride Sean *That Day's Struggle* p. 57.
[120] . ibid.
[121] .ibid. p. 61.

Government was facing. Who better to tell it in Paris than Maud? Her concern also was to publicize the plight of Catholics suffering pogroms in the North. Many refugees had been brought to Dublin by the I.R.A. to try and embarrass the new Government. Maud had looked to Griffith for assistance for them but he had refused. Maud found it difficult to realize that for the common good, difficult short term decisions had to be made sometimes.

It was in Paris Maud heard that the Free State Government had started to shell the Four Courts, with guns loaned by the British. She knew it was the start of a Civil War. She also knew her son and Catalina were in the Four Courts and in mortal danger. As she arrived in Dublin the battle raged on. Maud set up a Women's Committee to try to get peace. But the shelling set the buildings on fire and the occupiers surrendered on 30 June. They were taken to Mountjoy Jail. Hostilities continued in the city and country. The Women's Committee formed two delegations, one to speak to the Government, the other to the I.R.A. They proposed that a ceasefire occur and all personnel return home without being arrested and the prisoners released, until the Dail met and sorted the mess out.

On 1 July a delegation of women led by Maud and including Charlotte Despard, Louie Bennett, Agnes O'Farrelly, and Gertrude Webb went to see the Government. The Government was in continuous emergency session desperately trying to stay in control of a chaotic situation. They sent an official to see the women. Maud insisted on seeing Griffith. She berated him, pleading on behalf of those young idealistic men like her own son who fought the British and were now being hounded down or in jail. It was a pathetic scene for the two people who had known each other for so long, who had done so much together. Griffith, who like so many had loved Maud, was very ill and heartbroken[122]. But the Government had to stick together. He had to be strong. He had not come so far in the cause of Irish Nationalism to let a crowd of hotheads plunge the country back into British control. The response of Collins, Cosgrave and Griffith was that the Irregulars must surrender. Being very

---

[122] .Jordan Anthony J. *Arthur Griffith with James Joyce & WB Yeats Liberating Ireland*. Westport 2013 p.176-7.

proper/even with Maud, Griffith said "*We are a Government now and we have to keep order*"[123]. Louie Bennett wrote of the meeting; *Collins was excited, obviously excited. Griffith was utterly depressed; an old broken man. Cosgrave was outwardly unmoved, frigidly cold. Without the laying down of arms they would not negotiate[124]*". Hostilities continued.

This was a turning point for Maud. She decided that she would ally herself more closely with her own son and the other prisoners as he became the most important man in her life. Sean "*had learned from Mother that Griffith was an important nationalist*" but Sean always identified him as one who "*for whom all the older people had tremendous respect for but one would compromise, who would accept something much less than complete freedom or independence*"[125] She opened her house as a casualty center for Republicans. She was finished with the Government side. Very shortly her son-in-law Francis Stuart, Iseult's husband, was also arrested.

Matters deteriorated drastically when the Government began to execute some of its prisoners. The I.R.A. retaliated by shooting a Government Deputy. Arthur Griffith died suddenly from a stroke. His was the first funeral of an Irish Head of State. Ten days later Michael Collins was shot dead in an ambush. This left the Government under the control of W.T. Cosgrave, Kevin O'Higgins and General Richard Mulcahy. Martial Law was introduced. A new constitution was presented. Three hundred women prisoners were held in Kilmainham jail. Some including Mary Mac Sweeney, Grace Plunkett, Nora Connolly went on hunger strike. Many thousands of men were in prison, often in shocking conditions. Catalina Bulfin was jailed for one year in Kilmainham.

---

[123]. Jordan Anthony J. *Sean – A Biography of Sean MacBride* Blackwater Press 1993. P. 34.
[124]. Ward Margaret, Maud Gonne p. 133.
[125]. MacBride Sean, *That Day's Struggle, A Memoir 1904-1951* Curragh Press 2005. Edited By Caitriona Lawlor pp.37 & 45.

Maud along with Charlotte Despard set up the *Women's Prisoners Defense League (W.P.D.L.)*. They begin to agitate. They held meetings and went on deputations to Local Authorities. They visited jails and got as much publicity as possible. They came to be referred to as *"The Mothers"*. The Government tried to intimidate them. One of their meetings was shot at by the Army and many attending wounded. Maud's house was raided and most of her papers including letters from Yeats, Griffith and many more Irish figures were burned by the soldiers. Constance Markievcz was again arrested. But the Government was reluctant to arrest Maud herself, who now moved house with Charlotte Despard out of the city, to Roebuck House in Clonskeagh, a few miles from the city center.

One morning in Mountjoy Sean McBride and four leaders of the Four Courts Garrison were awoken very early and told to dress. The four were Liam Mellowes, Rory O'Connor, Richard Barrett, and Joseph McKelvey. They were told they were about to be shot. MacBride was returned to his cell, where he heard the fatal shots ring out.

deValera, O'Higgins, O'Connor wedding party.

The order had come from Kevin O'Higgins, whose *'Best Man' less* than one year previously had been Rory O'Connor. No more Government Deputies were murdered. The country was numbed by the execution of the four. But a clear message went out that the Government was determined to rule. The Civil War continued and the bitterness grew greater. The Anti-Treaty side under De Valera refused to participate in the Dail or organs of Government. They became outsiders to the new system.

The Government set up a second House of Parliament -The Senate - where representatives of various minorities and sectional interests could sit. Many of Maud's former friends and colleagues particularly from the Anglo-Irish set became senators. These included Andrew Jameson in whose house Maud had first stayed and Jennie Wyse-Power, a founder member of "*Inghini Na hEireann*. But the unkindest cut of all for Maud came when Willie Yeats accepted a nomination. Maud felt this as a betrayal against those who still wanted to fight for a Republic. But the old days when he would her bidding were past. Their paths had diverted and he was no longer influenced by her. He regretted this but accepted it as an unescapable fact. She told him she wouldn't have anything further to do with him, if he didn't resign his seat. Nancy Cardozo writes: *"For more than ten years Maud refused to see Willie. Even after he left the Senate, his support and semiofficial association with the Free State enraged her"* [126].

Yeats was pleased with the honor that being appointed to the Senate conferred upon him. He took his role very seriously contributing frequently to debates. He had to endure police protection for his house in Merrion Square as the houses of 37 Senators were burned down.

Willie was shortly to win international acclaim tor himself and his country when, after being nominated several times previously, he was awarded the Nobel Prize for Literature in 1923. When he was first told that he had won the Prize he immediately asked, *"How much, now much is it worth?* He travelled to Stockholm with his wife for the Award Ceremony. His patrician manner impressed everybody especially the Swedish Royal Family. This brought him £7,000, an enormous sum. Maud offered no congratulations. The award was for

---

[126] . Cardozo Nancy *Maud Gonne Gollancz 1979*. Ob.cit. p. 382.

his own work but also for the Literary Movement he had nurtured[127].

George & Willie Yeats.

The Government banned Maud's W.P.D.L. and lodged her in Kilmainham Jail. Now Iseult was the only member of the family free. She appealed to Yeats for help. Charlotte Despard started a vigil outside the jail. Inside Maud went on hunger strike with others. She was surprised to find she could do it. Yeats told the Government that Maud was aged 57 and couldn't survive very long, The Government, warning that it wouldn't be blackmailed again by hunger strikers, released Maud after 20 days. It gradually released the other hunger striking women.

The W.P.D.L. continued to hold public meetings, harassing the weary Government. A hunger strike began among the men in Mountjoy. But after two deaths, the prisoners gave in, realizing the Government would let them all die. Gradually men began to be released. The overcrowded conditions in Mountjoy were being eased by transferring men to Kilmainham. During one such operation, Sean McBride escaped from an ambulance and disappeared in the city streets. He met Maud briefly before going underground. She was so proud of him but afraid he might be shot. Roebuck House was now a major center for refugees and prisoners trying to rehabilitate themselves. It housed workshops and manufacturing units. Francis Stuart was released. Yeats would sometimes visit Iseult there. Maud always remained out of his company during his

---

[127] . *WB Yeats* by Anthony J. Jordan ob.cit. pp.162-4.

calls. Her image still cropped up in his work, comparing her early beauty to her present condition, *"Hollow of Cheek as though it drank the wind"*. Yeats served as a Senator of the new State for two four year terms 1922-1930.He played an active role, speaking often in the chamber. He tried, unsuccessfully, to create an open liberal society in the fledgling state.

Kevin O'Higgins, the Minister for Justice, and regarded as the main power force in the Government, was assassinated in 1927. Yeats had a great admiration for him as he knew of the crucial job he did in maintaining order. Among the terrible events O'Higgins had to justify was the execution of seventy seven republicans by the Irish Free State Army. His own Father had been shot dead at his home by republican raiders in 1923. Yeats writes that O'Higgins knew he was a target for assassination. He lived with the expectation of sudden death. But he was a great man who did not let that interfere with doing his duty.

Among those arrested for the murder was Sean MacBride. Luckily for Sean he had a cast iron alibi or else he might have faced execution[128]. He had spoken to a member of the Free State Government Party, Major Bryan Cooper on a ferry at the time of the murder, affording him an alibi. Sean was not released but jailed in Mountjoy for several weeks under the Public Safety Act. Sean had married his girlfriend, Catalina Bulfin on 26 January1926 on his 25th birthday, at 6 am in University Church on St Stephen's Green. He was still on the run and living in Sandymount. They went to Paris and later London before returning home[129].

As usual, despite the political stand-off between Maud and Yeats, when matters deteriorated in her family Maud turned to Willie for help, exchanging several long letters during 1927. She protested against Sean's arrest regarding it as victimization by the Free State giving personal details of Sean's family and business life. She wrote, *"The Free State now punishes those who fought England & honors ex Black & Tans. Of course Sean and I are Republicans. Ireland has a*

---

[128] . Jordan Anthony J. *Eamon deValera*, Westport Books, 2010. P. 145.
[129] . MacBride Sean, *That Day's Struggle* p. 100.

right to be independent. You believed that once long ago - but what is the use of writing this long letter to you who by your vote made yourself responsible for the Public Safety Act & put police above the magistrates & made law a mockery & derision. In the Public Safety Act the Free State legislators have given their measure. They will be remembered by it for all time[130].

Yeats responded after trying to intercede on Sean's behalf. He assured Maud that the Heads of the Free State did not want to be unjust to the son of Major John MacBride, whom they regarded as a hero. He told her that WT Cosgrave had been in the cell beside her husband was next to have been executed in Kilmainham. Yeats added, *"You are right- I think- in saying I was once a republican"*. Maud responded questioning his sincerity saying that his role *"leads you to vote for flogging Bills & Treasury Acts & Public Safety Acts. It leads me to found the WPDL"*. Yeats later told Maud, who had an accident and wanted to have a parole visit from Sean, that he *"offered to be personally responsible for your son. To go with him to Roebuck House, to wait there for him & to bring him back – I am sorry it was useless. It was the best I could do.* Willie told Maud *"We will never change each other's politics. They are too deeply rooted in our characters"*.

When Maud heard of Yeats' illness through Iseult, she wrote *"Go away into the Sun & reflect, write poetry & pray to God to send men who understand what love of Ireland & of their fellows' means to undo this mischief you– unwillingly perhaps have helped to do. For your poetry you will be forgiven, but sin no more"*.

Sean was later appointed was Director of Intelligence for the I.R.A. and later still in June 1936, Chief of Staff[131]. He seldom stayed at Roebuck House as it was raided frequently. Later Sean was able to move in with his mother. She was happy to have him and his beautiful Argentinian born wife, Kid Bulfin, with her. They were to have two children Anna and Tiernan, grandchildren for Maud. Sean worked for

---

[130] . *Gonne – Yeats Letters* 28 Sept. 1927 p. 433.
[131] .MacBride Sean, That Day's Struggle p. 121.

a time for the *Evening Telegraph*. That was his only source of income *"apart from Mother, who had an income of her own and was very generous"*[132]

It was rather ironic that Sean was accused of Kevin O'Higgins' murder as O'Higgins had been a great admirer of Sean's father. He wrote a contemporary poem on his execution:

'HOW HE DIED'

BY KEVIN CHRISTOPHER HIGGINS
(Courtesy of Una Higgins O'Malley)

I never was greatly a friend to John MacBride
But he caught my heart in the end by the death he died, Rich be his sleep and deep
By Kilmainham side!

For when they called him out, the cold last tryst to abide,
The cheeks of some of the men, though their hearts were stout
Had marked the ebb of the tide
And - set your lips as you can -
To riddle a smiling man is not, on the present plan
So perfectly cut and dried,
But it takes a bit of stiffening out of a soldier's pride!

Then in a cheery voice
As to friends at his side
'Lads' said the rebel 'I know if you had the choice
You'd let the thing abide
For you see, though my hands aren't tied,
I'd be giving away too much if 'twas fighting I tried
But the business has to be done
Though it isn't good fun.
Let you rest well o' nights; I will do it for one
And tell them nobody cried!

---

[132] .ibid p. 117

'Now some of you decent chaps
Aren't wonderful shots perhaps
But I'm not much further off than a hop and a stride
So you'll hit with the blessing of God
Or it is odd' said the rebel MacBride.

And when they thought anon
Of putting a bandage on
He moved aside -
'No' said John
There's nothing you need to hide
Right or wrong.

I've drunk my tea pretty strong
And faith! I've stared down life's barrels so long
I can do with the talk of a few of them open-eyed.'
'Just a moment 'he said'
'Wait till I bow my head
Then you can put me to bed'.
He bowed his head - and then he died.

So while I was never your friend,
Old John MacBride,
You caught my heart in the end
By the death you died;
Deep be the sleep you keep
By Kilmainham's side![133]

---

[133] . Una O'Higgins-O'Malley the daughter of Kevin O'Higgins provided the text of this poem to the author. She dates it as contemporary to 1916 as her father is using the spelling '*Higgins*' rather than the later version of '*O'Higgins*'.

Kevin O'Higgins

De Valera seeing that he and the country were going nowhere, decided to set up a new political party called *Fianna Fail*[134]. Many of the Anti-Treaty Republican side joined it, including many of Maud's women friends. But many of the I.R.A. diehards did not, including Sean McBride. Neither did his mother who now followed her son's lead in political matters. The new party did very well in the General Election, but WT Cosgrave held on to power. Constance Markievcz was one of the new Fianna Fail Deputies. A few days after the Election, she was rushed to Sir Patrick's Dunn's hospital where, in a public ward she died from an appendectomy. Her husband Casimir had come from Warsaw to be with her. The Government refused permissiom for her body to lie in State. Maud Gonne McBride's W.P.D.L. provided a guard of honor at Glasnevin Cemetery, where de Valera gave the oration.

Still the intimidation, the shootings, the reprisals continued in the country. A new body called 'Comhairle na Poblachta" was formed to unite all the republicans who remained outside Fianna Fail. Maud together with Sean joined this group. But it was short lived and

---

[134] . Jordan Anthony J.*Eamon deValera 1882-1975*, Westport 2010. Pp 137-158.

unsuccessful. Sean MacBride was again arrested and charged with treason Mr. Justice Hanna in trying McBride, held that the police had no right to arrest people on mere suspicion, nor did papers prove guilt. Arrested I.R.A. people began to sue the police for false arrest. The Commissioner for police was furious at this decision saying that now the police could only harass and watch these subversives. Suddenly life became more easy for extreme republicans, though Maud's house was raided shortly afterwards.

New Organizations proliferated. A new one which attracted little support and much criticism and harassment in 1931 was - *Saor Eire* -a left wing Republican grouping which had Helena Moloney and Sean McBride on its executive. The Government banned it, together with the *I.R.A., Cumann na mBan, W.P.D.L. Friends of Soviet Russia, Revolutionary Workers.* Maud's group, *WPDL* was evicted from their offices. They changed their name and continued to function and hold public meetings, demanding the release of all Republican prisoners. A Public Safety Order Act was passed giving police power to detain and search anyone. Sean MacBride himself became public enemy number one of the State security forces.

Chapter   18.

QUARRELS IN OLD AGE

Eamon De Valera had been born in New York City to a mother from Limerick and a Spanish father, who died when the boy was 2. He was reared by his grandmother in Limerick. He was jailed after the 1916 Rising and elected M.P. in 1917. He made a daring escape from Lincoln prison and was elected President of the First Dail. He worked closely with Arthur Griffith in Sinn Fein but opposed the Treaty. He was torn between the physical force Republicans and constitutional politics. He proved a tenacious politician, wily and difficult to pin down. In 1932 his new party, Fianna Fail won the 1932 General Election. The side that lost the Civil War was about to take over the Government from their most bitter enemies. Everyone held their breaths, but the transition occurred peacefully. The new Government's first action was to release all the political prisoners. A crowd of 30,000 waited to greet them in College Green. On the platform were Sean McBride and Maud Gonne McBride. Maud cautioned the crowd, *"We must remember that while the day of coercion has passed for a time, the task we have set ourselves has not yet been achieved"*[135].

Maud had high hopes for the new Government which moved swiftly to stop paying land annuities to Britain and tried to make the country self-sufficient. De Valera abolished or suspended several public order laws. He told the I.R.A. that there was no longer any reason for their continued existence. They should join their old civil war comrades in the National Army. Sean McBride was offered the rank of Major General in the Army by the ex I.R.A. Chief of Staff, and then Minister for Defense, Frank Aiken. Sean was insulted by the offer and rejected it immediately. Sean was subsequently offered

---

[135] . Jordan Anthony J. *Eamon deValera 1882-1975. Irish; Catholic; Visionary.* Westport 2010. P.178.

a job as a subeditor with the Irish Press. It was his first full-time job and he hated it and resigned feeling either by ambition or temperament that he was meant for greater things. The I.R.A. believed that it had a legitimate right to exist independently of the State and began to operate openly harassing members of the defeated Government. A Para Military Force was set up to protect the Opposition and was called the *Blue Shirts*. Conflict arose quickly between it and the I.R.A. with the official security force looking on.

DeValera entered discussions with the IRA over the next eighteen months to explore their mutual positions. DeValera's position was that majority rule had to be accepted. Sean MacBride represented the IRA and told deValera that he did not accept that position in 1916 nor in 1926 and that majority rule was laudable for a free people. These discussions went nowhere and led to some suspicion among the IRA, who knew that at an earlier time MacBride had acted as secretary to DeValera. Sean reported on Dev, *"He is a very hard person to argue with and I found it extremely hard to get him to consider anything except his own point of view"[136]*.

Three months after announcing the disbandment of her *W.P.D.L.* Maud resurrected it saying the secret police were again as bad as ever in harassing activists. Cumann na mBan launched an Anti-British goods campaign. de Valera called a snap election and won a larger and safer mandate. He announced that no group in the country had the right to carry arms except the official forces. He sacked the Chief of Police Eoin O'Duffy and reintroduced a Military Tribunal to deal with the worsening security situation. Maud criticized this action publicly, asking had Fianna Fail forgotten. De Valera showed little sign of declaring an Irish Republic, which Maud and many like her who had supported him, expected. Maud campaigned for pensions for those who had fought for the republican cause. In 1932 she applied for a pension herself, as the widow of her executed husband, Major John MacBride. She was

---

[136] . Jordan, *DeValera* p. 200

requested to provide documentary proof of the marriage. Her reply reads:

Roebuck House
Clonskeagh
Phone Dundrum 25

A Chara,
I am returning the application form filled in.
I have written to Paris for a copy of the certificate of my marriage
and will forward it on receipt.
I remain
Sincerely Yours
Maud Gonne MacBride

Reference: IE/MA/MSPC/DP6639 — John MacBride

Maud was awarded £22 in 1933 after she provided a copy of her marriage certificate. Hew award was cut as she had not applied under the 1923 Act. She later received £67. 10 shillings, rather than £90. After a new military pension law was passed in 1937 she received an increased payment, as Madame Gonne MacBride[137].

Willie began to write to Maud again and she replied. They began to meet occasionally. But as usual they were very prone to arguing. They tried to steer clear of politics, which was a difficult task. Yeats was an elitist and Maud a populist. Yeats had begun to feel that the country needed strong government,
even a dictatorship. He almost hoped that the Commissioner of Police, O'Duffy would have organised a coup and dismissed DeValera prior to deValera dismissing him. A period of ten years had elapsed without them meeting, though Willie kept in touch with Iseult, whom he came to regard as his daughter. Willie went to live in London again where he was busy with his own life, having two children, an adoring wife and

---

[137]. Military Pensions Archives

an adoring public to contend with. Later he later moved back to Dublin to live near the site of Pearse's School in Rathfarnham. There he began to talk about creating an Irish Renaissance by gathering the best minds together into one group - an *Irish Academy of Culture*. This he succeeded in doing with some of Maud's contemporaries like George Russell and George Bernard Shaw and James Stephens. It also included Francis Stuart, though James Joyce ungraciously refused an invitation[138]. Maud was very interested to see Yeats at work again in Ireland, especially as the authorities attacked his group. Strict censorship was in force with many literary works banned. This disheartened James Joyce in Paris and caused him further disillusionment with the new State. Had Arthur Griffith, a defender of James Joyce against censorship, lived this conservatism would scarcely have occurred.

Yeats decided to write briefly about the current situation. He knew that he and others had failed in their efforts to ensure that Irish society would be open-minded. He felt that his years in *The Senate* had almost been a waste of time. It suited political and church leaders to create an introverted and parochial society. Writers were treated with contempt. He wrote that maybe the Church and State had succeeded in cowering their subjects. He believed religion should be life giving. If the worst had happened and Church and State became oppressors, then it bode badly for religion and politics.

CHURCH AND STATE

Here is fresh matter, poet,
Matter for old age meet;
Might of the Church and the State,
Their mobs put under their feet.
O but heart's wine shall run pure,
Mind's bread grow sweet.

That were a cowardly song,
Wander in dreams no more;

---

[138] . Jordan Anthony J. *James Joyce Unplugged*. Westport 2017 p. 166.

What if the Church and State
Are the mob that howls at the door?
Wine shall run thick to the end,
Bread taste sour.

Willie Yeats had resigned from the Senate some years earlier, which meant he was no longer part of the State apparatus, Maud came to hate. But she was very slow to contemplate forgiving him. He wrote about their quarrel in old age due to his supporting the new State. He asked where her sweetness gone? He believed that her mind had been poisoned towards him by enemies. He felt that one who had accepted old age, had accepted enough. Old age conferred some wisdom. He was sure that despite what had happened between them, she once was as beautiful to him as the Spring itself.

QUARRELS IN OLD AGE

Where had her sweetness gone?
* What fanatics invent*
* In this blind bitter town*
* Fantasy or incident*
* Not worth thinking of,*
* Put her in a rage.*
* I had forgiven enough*
* That had forgiven old age.*

Many of Maud's old women associates decided to mark her service of 50 years to the cause of Ireland and especially the cause of freeing prisoners. She was embarrassed and tried to dissuade them. But they went ahead and she was publicly honored by them. Many ex-prisoners and members of the *W.P.D.L.* attended.

Charlotte Despard & Maud Gonne

Helena Moloney was one of the main speakers. Maud passed off what she had done lightly but warned her audience against complacency. *'The jails are still there'* she reminded them, *'there is still no Irish Republic'*. Maud's great friend Charlotte Despard had gone to work in Belfast where anti-Catholic pogroms were continuing. Maud who knew the North well from the days of the *Shan Van Vocht*, travelled northwards to lend her support. She gave a few lectures and was then arrested during the night in Lurgan and expelled to the South. Conor Cruise O'Brien described Maud as *"in her dramatic widow's weeds, tall and gaunt, towering over her tiny pugnacious friend, Madame Despard, Lord French's sister"*[139].The indignity and injustice of Partition appalled her.

Maud and Sean spoke at an I.R.A. sponsored rally in College Green. A new *Republican Congress* was formed but it split and many of its members went off to fight in the Spanish Civil War. The I.R.A. began to get involved in trade disputes; they were also active in the North, all causing problems for the Government. De Valera finally started interning Republicans. The I.R.A. launched a new political party - *The Republican Party of Ireland-* Sean McBride was the man mainly responsible. Maud stood for the party in local elections but was defeated along with all its other candidates. De Valera finally decided he had had enough of his former comrades. Using the same powers as the Cosgrave Government had, he banned the I.R.A. and its paper "*An*

---

[139]. States of Ireland Conor Cruise O'Brien Panther 1974. P. 111.

Phoblacht". The prisons began to fill again with Republicans. Though past 70 years, Maud took to the streets again with her WPDL. Hunger strikes commenced. Sean MacBride, who had recently completed his legal studies, was again on the run, though resigning from holding the position of Chief of Staff of the IRA. Maud produced a news sheet called - *Prison Bars* - detailing the conditions within the jails. She was now closely linked with her son's faction of the I.R.A. She didn't recognize the legitimacy of the State. Yet she attended a reunion of the *White Cross* Council at the Mansion House which many of her female colleagues refused to attend, owing to the presence cf De Valera.

DeValera decided to replace the 1922 Constitution with one of his own. He abolished the *Irish Free State* and introduced Eire or Ireland, though not as a Republic. Its introduction led to much friction because of its Catholic ethos. Many women objected to its view of women. Maud gave over a full edition of *"Prison Bars"* to attack it. An article by Hanna Sheehy Skeffington said, *"Never before have women been so united, as now when they are faced with Fascist proposals endangering their livelihood, cutting away their rights as human beings. Mr. DeValera shows mawkish distrust of women which has always coloured his outlook...He has refused to restore 1916 Equal Rights and Equal opportunities for women..."*[140]. There was an Irish President in the new Constitution. All the political parties agreed on the nomination of one of Maud's oldest admirers, Doughlas Hyde, a Protestant.

For several years Maud had thought about writing an account of her own life. After all, Willie Yeats had been doing it for years. Many people had encouraged her to put her memories down on paper. As well, there might be some money in it and the family was not then very well off. Her income fell drastically when true to her own principles she and Sean had converted the principal of her family money to Irish Government Bonds. The family would later become involved in selling tickets for the Irish Hospital Sweepstakes as a money making exercise. Maud wrote to Yeats telling him of her

---

[140] .Ward Margaret *Maud Gonne* p. 174.

plans to write a book and asking for his support as well as permission to quote his poetry. As usual Willie was forthright and clarified a few of her thoughts about his own attitude to Irish freedom.

Maud decided that the time was not yet right for her to be totally frank about her early life. Sean McBride had a life and a career ahead of him. Ireland was still very conservative where the strictures of the Church were paramount. The title she chose for the book - *A Servant of the Queen* - was very strange for most people so she had to go to great care in the book to explain it.

Most people assumed that it must be a monarch she was referring to when she used the word 'Queen', particularly her English audience. But Maud always saw Ireland as a Queen and she was one of her servants. She believed she had seen the mystical Ireland on some of her early trips in the West of Ireland. She decided to end her story at the time she got married to John MacBride. There was no point in reopening old wounds. There was no criticism of her husband in the book, rather was he portrayed as a gentle conservative man, trying to adapt to Maud's independent way. She wrote about how "*he was full of queer conventions*" and shocked at her suggestion that she could take tea in his tiny attic. Their mission to free Ireland united them. She had once told John O'Leary that she thought that by marrying John MacBride she was marrying Ireland [141] . She documents all the advice they both received not to marry, he from his mother and brother, she from Arthur Griffith and her father Tommy. The book was very well accepted, especially in Ireland, as a valuable documentary on a part of Irish social and political history. Later it was identified as containing much that was fictional and treated as unreliable for many factual matters.

On 7 October 1939 the Irish Ambassador to Germany William Warnock reported to Joseph P.Walshe in Dublin that *Madame Maud Gonne MacBride's 'Servant of the Queen' is ready for issue; this was, however, translated as a private venture of the German publisher. At*

---

[141] .O'Leary Papers NLI Ms. 800

first the Ministry withheld its sanction for the translation of 'Servant of the Queen', as the English publishers are Jewish, but once the responsible official had read the book he immediately gave permission. On 19 April he reported; Madame Maud Gonne MacBride's autobiography, 'Servant of the Queen', was translated into German, and had a large sale[142].

Yeats, whose health was deteriorating, never got round to reading Maud's book. But the pair still visited each other. Willie still thought she was the most beautiful woman he had encountered. He still marveled at her adherence to the republican cause. That winter of 1938 Willie went to the South of France for the heat. There on January 28th 1939 he died at Cap Martin outside the walls of Monaco. Iseult wrote to her friend George Yeats, bemoaning that they had both suffered a terrible loss in his growing old and dying. Maud recalled her favorite poem of his *"Red Hanrahan's Song"*.

At the end of that same year another old friend of Maud's died, Charlotte Despard. She was buried in the Republican plot in Glasnevin. Maud gave the funeral tribute. She had been President of the W.P.D.L. all those years.

The outbreak of the Second World War put most Irish Nationalists in a peculiar position. This was England's difficulty again. Maud was very old and confined for the most part to writing her views to the papers. There was much Pro-German sentiment in Dublin. The German Embassy remained open during the war. The Ambassador was a guest at Roebuck House. Francis Stuart was offered a post in the University at Berlin and accepted it, leaving Iseult and their two children behind. Stuart had some involvement in seeking German help for Ireland. A German officer parachuted into Wicklow and tried to make contact with Iseult who was supposed to help him contact the I.R.A. The German was captured and Iseult arrested but later released. The Government was very wary of 'German Plots' and tried to stay strictly neutral during the War while at the same time cooperating with the Allies on the ground. Republicans were again interned. The old

---

[142]. No. 48 NAI DFA 219/4

cycle of shootings, reprisals were occurring again. This time Sean McBride, Senior Counsel, was defending them in court, where possible. Military Tribunals were again in session. The I.R.A. had been mounting a bombing campaign in England and De Valera was under pressure to contain them. The prisons overflowed and a compound was opened at the Curragh Army Camp. The hard cases were confined to Portlaoise Prison. The I.R.A. was again at war with De Valera's Government.

A son of Tomas MacCurtain, who as Lord Mayor of Cork, had been assassinated by the British in 1920, was sentenced to death on 13 June 1940. Sean T. O'Kelly Minister for Finance liaised with Sean MacBride and provided legal information to enable MacBride to postpone and hopefully thwart the imminent execution. The Registrar of the Supreme Court was Con Curran whom MacBride describes, *"He was a writer also, quite well known during the period, a literary figure in Dublin"*. MacBride carried out his legal maneuvers and told O'Kelly, *"Well now, I've done what you asked me to do. It's over to you. I won't be able to do it again. There'll be an appeal and it'll be dismissed"*. So Sean T. O'Kelly went to bat and finally the government, by a majority, overturned its earlier decision, and reprieved MacCurtain on 10 July 1940[143].

Prison conditions were shocking with hunger strikers going naked for months. The prisoners claimed political status but the Government treated them as criminals. The most infamous case surrounded Sean McCaughey, whom Sean defended. Maud wrote to the Press.

To the editor of the *Irish Times*

Sir— Those unable to serve can demand nothing; therefore, I, who am almost 80 and bedridden, make my last request ... I make it to the people and to the Government: Let no more young lives be sacrificed to uphold an old British rule of Victorian origin; be speedier than death in releasing young McCaughey; please, with him, release the others from

---

[143] . Sean MacBride *That Day's Struggle* Editd by Caitriona Lawor 2005 p 128-129.

Portlaog-hise Jail who have been fighting that old British rule with the same spirit of courage and endurance which liberated twenty-six of our counties and among whom is the son of our comrade Lord Mayor McCurtin, who, dying for Ireland, entrusted his own children to her care. Only when this is done can our Government and people unitedly, without hypocrisy, demand that the ill treatment of prisoners in our six occupied counties shall cease.

CLANN AN POBLACHTA

MOTHER AND SON ENTER LEINSTER HOUSE

DECLARATION OF AN IRISH REPUBLIC

Maud Gonne, Sean MacBride, Louie O'Brien.

The end of the War in 1945 brought another reminder of the international dimension to Maud's work as the Indian Irish League formally dissolved. The remaining cash was presented to the Cambridge University Indian Fund for £98 .The presentation was made by Maud Gonne.

As the deValera Government became unpopular, Sean McBride decided to seize the initiative and set up a new political party - *Clan na Poblachta-* (Republican Family) in 1946 to galvanize republican support against the Government. A massive release of the prisoners was mounted. The I.R.A. said it would expel any of its members who joined the new Party which won two sensational bye Elections. Sean McBride accompanied by his mother, entered Leinster House to take his seat in an Irish Parliament[144]. It brought to her mind how she had accompanied Lucien Millevoye to take his seat in the Chamber of Deputies in Paris more than fifty years earlier. deValera panicked. He called a snap Election and lost. *Clann na Poblachta* with ten seats, helped to form a new Coalition Government with its bitter enemies, from the first Free State Government. Maud Gonne McBride kept her own counsel as Sean McBride became *Minister for External Affairs*. One of the hall-marks of the new Government was to demonstrate its *'filial loyalty'* to the Holy See, just as deValera's Governments had done.

The next year the new Government declared an *Irish Republic*. It was proclaimed on the anniversary of the 1916 Easter Rising, on Easter Monday 1949. Maud accompanied her son to the Solemn High Mass and *Te Deum* in Dublin's Pro Cathedral[145]. One of her greatest wishes had come true, thanks in no small way to her son. They had kept the faith.

There has been much speculation about the exact role played by Sean MacBride in this development. His private secretary was in no doubt as she wrote to me in 1992. I had earlier interviewed Louie O'Brien, unpaid Private Secretary to Sean MacBride, during his time as Minister, for my 1993 biography of Sean. After separation from her husband she and her son Conal lived in Roebuck House with the MacBride's. In 1991 controversy had resurfaced over whether a journalist named Hector Legge of the Sunday Independent had leaked the news about the declaration of the Republic to force Costello to make a premature announcement about it while on a visit to Canada in 1948. Legge and Louie O'Brien exchanged letters in the Irish Times in December 1991 and January 1992. This led me to make contact again with Louie. She subsequently wrote to me about this and other more personal issues[146]. Her letter of 16 February 1992 reads:

Garden Flat 8
51 Pembroke Road

---

[144]. Cardozo Nancy, ob. Cit. p. 401.
[145]. Jordan Anthony J. Sean MacBride A Biography, p. 113.
[146]. Jordan *Sean*, p. 107.

D.4.

Dear Tony,

I feel I have to explain about the MacBride-Noel Browne conversations in the Russell Hotel......

As to Sean's has sent a memorandum to Costello in Canada; one has to remember that we did not know that it was Sean who had leaked the information to Legge. We were all disgusted that it could happen – including Sean joining in! It was a long time afterwards that I learned the truth – from the newspaper man that Sean had chosen to leak the misinformation to Legge. Afterwards I was able to believe that it was Sean who had set out Costello's options. It was the first glimpse I got of the feet of clay!

So many dishonest and dishonorable acts followed with the years that I became totally disillusioned...

Louie OB`

Sean MacBride was Vice-President of the Organisation for European Economic Co-operation from 1948-1951 and was President of the Committee of Ministers of the Council from 1948-9. During this period he was a sponsor and signatory of four major international accords; the Convention for European Economic Cooperation (Paris 1948), the Statute of the Council of Europe (London 1949), the Geneva Convention for the Protection of War Victims (1949) and the European Convention of Human Rights (Rome 1950). He told Dail Eireann what he hoped for with the Council of Europe; *it is in my view, one of the most important and constructive developments that have taken place in Europe. I hope it will evolve rapidly into a more closely-knit body that may lead to a Federated States of Europe...it excludes from its ambit all questions of military measures. Unlike many other attempts at world organizations, it relies rather on moral, ethical, social and economic forces than upon military measures. I have pleasure in asking the House to ratify the Statute.*

His mother could not but be proud to see her son carry on her own inheritance in an international sphere.

Chapter 19

SEAN MACBRIDE FACILITATES REPATRIATION

OF WB YEATS

In one of the last letters Maud wrote to Yeats, she had said, "*Oh how you hate old age - well so do I. I see no redeeming features in it, but I, who am more a rebel against man than you, rebel less against nature, & accept the inevitable & go with it gently into the unknown—only against the sordidness & cruelty of small ambitions I fight until the long rest comes—out of that rest I believe the Great Maker will refashion great beauty & life again. While we sleep she will work in the stupendous energy of Creation—but till sleep comes our souls and bodies fight—in weariness, which is old age—at the awakening it will be with the glory & joy of youth again*[147].

Maud Gonne was one of those who were most anxious that Yeats' remains be returned to Ireland. She wrote to another old friend, President Douglas Hyde, to Eamon deValera and to FR Higgins at the Abbey Theatre. The latter assured her that "*We are making every endeavor to have the remains back to Ireland*"[148].Little did Maud realize that it would be her own son who would in fact be the champion of returning Yeats' remains after the War, as Minister of

---

[147] . *Gonne-Yeats Letters p.*445-6
[148] . *The Yeats Gonne Letters*, Edited by Anna MacBride White & A. Noran Jeffares   Pimlico 1993.pp. 453-4.

External Affairs in an Irish Government. Both their French links easing officialdom in the process.

In my 2003 biography of WB Yeats, I wrote: *"When Willie died in the south of France in January 1939, Maud like many others was anxious that he be buried in Ireland. After the War preparations were made to repatriate Willie's remains back to Drumcliffe in Sligo, where he had wanted to be buried. It transpired that his grave at Roquebrune had been interfered with and his remains removed to another quarter of the cemetery. This happened despite George having bought a ten year plot in 1939. Attempts were made locally to dissuade the Yeats family from exhuming the remains, due to the uncertainty of their precise location. However external pressures on the family, and their own desire to have the remains re-interred at Sligo, necessitated that a somewhat uncertain exhumation went ahead"[149].*

Ann Saddlemyer writes *"George wrote to the French Ambassador in Dublin [Ostrogg]. Within months the transfer had become a formal intergovernmental affair, no doubt encouraged by the Minister of External Affairs Sean MacBride, with whom George had several private discussions"[150].*

In more recent years documents from French Archives outline in some detail the circumstances surrounding the exhumation. Michael Yeats, the poet's son, sought official help in locating the poet's remains from Stanislas Ostrogu, French Ambassador in Dublin. Neither Michael Yeats not Sean MacBride, the Irish Foreign Minister, who organised the ceremony, wanted to know the details of how the remains were to be collected. Ostrogu repeatedly urged caution and discretion saying that the Irish Ambassador in Paris should not be informed. Sean MacBride had very close relations with Count Stanislaus Ostrorog, who had actually asked to be posted to Ireland. Sean writes that, *"I had very close relations with the French*

---

[149] . Jordan Anthony , *WB Yeats Vain;Glorious; Lout. A Maker of Modern Ireland*. Westport Books 2003. p. 114.
[150] . Saddlemeyer Ann, *Becoming George*, Oxford University Press 2002, p. 605.

Ambassador, Count Stanislaus Ostrorog. He was a charming man, most helpful to me always"[151]. Jacques Camille Paris[152], Europe Director Quai d'Orsay, responded to Ostrorog authorising use of the foreign minister's general fund to finance the return of Yeats' remains.

French diplomat Bernard Cailloux was assigned to investigate the possibility of repatriating Yeats' remains. He investigated the situation and made his report as follows:

It was necessary to know :

1.   If Mr Yeats was interred in the Cemetery in Roquebrune

2.   If his body was interred in a communal grave

3.   If it was possible to exhume his remains for a possible return

Having been asked to enquire into the questions listed above I am now pleased to report as follows:

1.   Mr William Butler Yeats died at the Hôtel Idéal-Séjour, Roquebrune (A. M.) on 28 January 1939. His death was certified by Mr Germon doctor in Roquebrune-Carnoles, Quartier de Bansstron, he was buried in the communal grave in Roquebrune.

2.   In January 1946, that is well after the time limit from the interment in the communal grave, he was exhumed and interred in the Ossuaire de Cimetiére. Of course this undertaking was not confined to the remains of Mr Yeats but also included the remains of many others buried in the same area of the communal grave.

---

[151]. MacBride Sean, That Day'sStruggle p.93 & 158.
[152]. It was Jacques Camille Paris who provided the newly available French documentation.

3.   The remains of Mr Yeats are still in the Ossuaire, mixed pell-mell with other bones. On an initial view it seems impossible to restore them to the natural order to which they belong. However, a meeting with the Abbé Biancheri, the parish priest of Roquebrune and Mr Lautier, the head gravedigger of the cemetery gave me the following information : a/ enquiries by the family of the deceased around three months ago established that Mr Yeats was wearing at the time of his death a corselet with truss and which wasn't pointed out to the gravedigger at the time and this was mentioned during the discussion, and Mr Lautier confirmed to me that he had seen an item of this type in the grave in the course of the work, as well as a large skull with false teeth ? Was it really the remains of the deceased?

4.   I looked to obtain confirmation on this point. First of all, it appears that there is nobody still in the country who knew Mr Yeats well. The former owners of the Hôtel Idéal-Séjour (Mr and Mrs Ménard, avenue Bedoux á Roquebrune) have only a vague memory of their former client : they could only confirm the general information already known : a tall man, a large head, paralysed in both arms . . . . similarly, the former staff of the hotel are now dispersed at unknown addresses.

In the course of my researches, I found that the doctor who looked after Mr Yeats was an English doctor living in Monte-Carlo ; but without any information on his identity I was not able to go to see him. Similarly in relation to Dr Germon, while I was able to meet him, he had no memory of his client for whom he only provided a death certificate. His only memory of the deceased was he had a religious book in his hands, probably the Bible.

In Summary :

A   It is impossible to recover all the remains of Mr Yeats

B   As a result of enquiries carried out by the family it would be possible to recover a corselet of iron, a cranium box , and possibly a Bible.

C   If the restoration of these objects suffice or if it was essential that a full body be restored, Mr Rebouillat, the forsenic doctor in Roquebrune would be able to restore a skeleton presenting all the characteristics of the deceased.

D   For the restoration of B/ or that of c/ the steps to be taken are those required by the funeral services in Menton (Maison Roblot) who have the specialised staff for these services and who can follow up as required with the Mayor of Roquebrune.

Signed :

CAILLOUX

Attached : copy of extract from Register of Deaths for Mr Yeats
            copy of death certificate.

Bernard Cailloux then wrote to Jacques Camille Paris, Europe Director Quai d'Orsay;"*I was most anxious to resolve the issue, for if the family and the Irish legation were obviously guilty of negligence, the French authorities could also be taken to task if it were known that this great foreign poet, who has spent many years of his life in France had been thrown into a communal grave*".

The certificate of exhumation by Dir. Rebouillat says that he and five other men who collected Yeats' remains in the ossuary were guided by "*the age, the size, the existence of an orthopedic corset and a denture*" He claims the identification was made "*with certainty and precision*" and notes that the bones were placed in a coffin which was "*closed, soldered and sealed in our presence*". However Cailloux concluded that "*evidence constitutes that the remains in the coffin sent to Ireland are not those of WB Yeats*".
Dr. Rebouillat's bill for 5,000 francs was paid by the foreign ministry general fund. When the Irish government later volunteered to

reimburse, a French diplomat wrote that the French Government ought to *"derive the moral benefit of having footed the bill"*.

Yeats's coffin is nailed down in Roquebrune

Ostrorog wrote that he *"summoned the young Yeats to inform him, without giving any details, that following an investigation, the mortal remains of his father had been collected and were currently in a coffin in Roquebrune cemetery.* He thanked me wholeheartedly, avoiding asking for any other explanation. *"*
A few weeks later, Ostrorog met MacBride, who *"expressed to me personally in the warmest terms his thanks for the care with which this affair had been resolved . . . We understood each other without it being spelled out. MacBride's mother was formerly extremely close to the poet. There was obviously an interest that no incident would happen that could give rise to a press campaign"*.

The plan was that the Le Macha would sail from Dunlaoire to Nice to collect the remains. In August 1948 George wrote to MacBride, *"you will see that the papers have got wind of the Corvette. Do let me have a date as soon as you can".The Macha sailed on 25 August calling to Gibraltar before arriving in Nice. On 6 September the* formal and warm courtesies were extended by the French who had given a military band guard of honor to Yeats' coffin as it was taken to the Macha from the cemetery at Roquebrune. At the quayside, trumpets were sounded, arms presented and the French and Irish national anthems were played as the coffin was taken on board and tied down on deck.

As the plane carrying Sean Murphy, Ireland's Ambassador to France, flew in to Nice, it crashed on landing but no injuries occurred. Murphy later wrote to Foreign Minister Robert Schuman on 21 February 1949 to express the Irish Government's gratitude.

Sir/Madam

I have the honour to inform your Excellency that the Irish government has requested me to convey its deepest gratitude to you for the help and all the facilities provided by the French authorities who willingly gave so much assistance last Sept during the exhumation and transfer of the mortal remains of the Irish poet William Butler Yeats from Roquebrune cemetery to Nice.

Yeats was one of the most illustrious men of letters that Ireland has had and the Irish government is very appreciative of the display of respect given to his remains, an honour which is befitting of the traditional friendship that has existed between our two countries for many years. The Irish Government feels that the deep respect and honour given to Yeats, an Irish poet whose last days were spent in France and whose remains lay in French soil for several years, have closely united our two countries who share cultural affinities

The homage shown as his remains left his much loved France to be brought back to his native country will not be forgotten for as long as Yeats lives on in the memory of Irish people

My Government is convinced that the honours bestowed on this occasion were bestowed not only on Yeats but also on Ireland and on the Irish people. Consequently the Irish Government wishes to thank firstly the French Government, all the public figures, local government officers and the French army and naval officers who at the cemetery and again in Nice organised and participated in ceremonies in memory of Yeats. I would especially like to convey the Irish Government's deepest gratitude to Monsieur Paris, European Director, Monsieur Benoist from the Department of foreign affairs, the state representative of the Alps- Maritimes department, the commander of the port of Nice and to the commander of the guard of honour for their valuable contribution.

The Irish Government also wishes to express its gratitude to the French for its generosity in covering the costs of transporting the poet's body from Roquebrune to Nice.

I take this opportunity to convey the assurances of my highest consideration to your Excellency[153].

The Le Macha took the remains to Galway from where they travelled to Sligo by road. The operation was overseen by Sean MacBride, Minister of External Affairs, who also represented his mother at the graveside in Drumcliffe. Maud was too weak to travel. Roy Foster writes, *"But with a curious symmetry, the government minister for External Affairs, closely involved throughout, was her son Sean MacBride, who in another age, had flown kites with WBY at Coleville and been given sanctuary by the newly married Yeats' at Ballinamantane thirty years before"[154]*.

The Irish State had intended to afford a State funeral but in deference to the poet's family, the only State ceremonial was the provision of a military guard of honor for the body on its arrival at Sligo. Jack Yeats insisted that there be no address or oration at the graveside. Sean MacBride represented the Government, himself and his mother, who among the large gathering at the graveside had probably known Yeats the longest[155].

> Under bare Ben Bulben's head
> In Drumcliffe churchyard Yeats is laid.
> An ancestor was rector there
> Long years ago, a church stands near,
> By the road an ancient cross.
> No marble, no conventional phrase;

---

[153]. No. 278. NAI /6/411/3/16 part 1

[154]. Foster Roy, *WB Yeats The Arch-Poet* Oxford University Press 2003. p. 657

[155]. Jordan Anthony J. , *WB Yeats, Vain; Glorious;Lout.* Westport 2007.

On limestone quarried near the spot
By his command these words are cut:

Cast a cold eye
On life, on death.
Horseman, pass by!

As a mark of gratitude George sent Sean MacBride one of her husband's manuscripts, making it clear that it was for him personally, *"for keeps"*. On 28 October at a ceremony on the Macha, Michael Yeats presented a portrait of his father to Lieutenant –General McKenna, Chief of Staff and officers of the Ship. Present were George, Jack, Anne, and Sean MacBride in his official capacity[156].

CONTROVERSY

Alfred Hollis, an Englishman who died around the same time as Yeats, and who was initially buried next to him, wore a steel corset for spinal tuberculosis. In his certificate of exhumation from March 20th, 1948, Rebouillat based his reconstitution of Yeats's skeleton on *"the presence of a thoracic corset"*. Yeats's son, Michael, said he wore a leather truss for a hernia. Hollis's family claimed that it was he, not Yeats, who was sent for burial in Sligo.

In her 1988 biography of Gluck, Diana Souhami recounted how in 1946, Edith Shackelton Heald, Yeats' last lover, had crouched on the floor of their hotel in Monte Carlo, sobbing after visiting the site of his burial, saying, *"I would know his bones anywhere"*. Later when they heard about the possible exhumation and repatriation they put out suggestions against such a course of action. The publication of the biography added to the controversy over whose body had been repatriated. Gluck recounted the painstaking research she had conducted and concluded that "these remains would be almost impossible to find, and if found, identity would be open to doubt". This forced the two children of the poet to become involved. This

---

[156] . George, p. 611.

they did by issuing a letter to the Irish Times on 6 October 1988. It read:

YEATS'S GRAVE

Sir, — In view of the publication last week in England of a book that refers to the grave of W. B. Yeats in Drumcliffe Cemetery, we wish on behalf of the Yeats family to make certain matters clear:

1. The suggestion that our father was buried in a paupers' grave in Roquebrune is of course totally untrue. The friends who attended the burial (were they still alive) could have testified to this, as do the documents and receipts relating to the funeral that are in our possession.

2. Our mother, Mrs George Yeats, in making the arrangements for the funeral in Roquebrune, made it clear to all concerned tha she intended later on to return the body of W. B. Yeats to Ireland. With this in mind she negotiated with various shipping lines, but matters dragged on due to legal and technical problems, so that ultimately it was necessary to leave matters over until after the war.

3. Mrs Yeats arranged with the French authorities to acquire a 10-year grave plot for her husband at Roquebrune. We should stress that she was an extremely able and efficient woman, speaking excellent French. She had for many years organised the business affairs of W. B. Yeats and was, in fact, the last person who would make any mistake on a matter of such crucial importance.

4. It appears that at some stage the body was moved. On hearing of this our mother at once got in touch with the French government authorities. Thenceforth she was kept informed by them of events at Roquebrune, and was therefore in a position to satisfy herself that there would be no problems associated with the transfer of the body back to Ireland.

5. In preparation for the ultimate transfer to Ireland, the remains were exhumed in March, 1948, and placed in a Chapel of Rest. Careful measurements were made of the remains (Yeats had a particularly massive bone structure), and the task of certification was made easier by the fact that, due to a long-term hernia problem, our father wore a truss.

6. The exhumation took place in full conformity with the rigorouss French laws on these matters, and in the presence of the Mayor of Roquebrune, senior police officials, a medical expert, the Superintendent of Graves, and other persons of expert and official standing. The presence of these officials and experts was designed to ensure in accordance with law that the indentity of the remains should be established beyond all possibility of error.

7. In September, 1948, the body of William Butler Yeats was brought home to Sligo and interred in the cemetery at Drumcliffe.

We regret that 40 years later it should be necessary for us to issue this statement about delicate matters that should normally be private family affairs. We hope it will not be necessary for us to contribute further to this discussions. There is, indeed, nothing to discuss since we are satisfied beyond doubt that our father's body is indeed buried in Drumcliffe Cemetery. — Yours, etc.,

ANNE YEATS,
MICHAEL YEATS,
Dalkey, Co. Dublin.

In my own biography of WB Yeats[157], I referred, in passing, to this controversy saying, "*External pressures on the family and their own desire to have the remains re-interred at Sligo, necessitated that a somewhat uncertain exhumation went ahead*". A lecture on the book I gave in Sligo led to a headline report on the front page of the *Irish Independent, Grave doubts surface over who lies in Yeats's tomb*. This was taken up by British and American media and reported as if this was my new theory. In the same vein a local newspaper in Sligo asked, '*Who is Anthony Jordan and why is he trying to destroy our tourist industry?*' In fact the sparse detail I had included in my book came from an inspection of the very skeptical contemporary reports of the exhumation, then on display in the local Museum in Sligo itself.

---

[157]. Jordan Anthony J., *WB Yeats Vain,Glorious, Lout. A Maker of Modern Ireland*. Westport Books 2003 p. 114

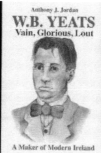

CHAPTER 20

SEAN MACBRIDE OPPOSES REPATRIATION

OF JAMES JOYCE

When the new Irish Government met in 1948, ending sixteen
continuous years rule by Eamon deValera's Fianna Fail, it decided to
send a telegram to the Pope desiring *'to repose at the feet of your
Holiness the assurance of our filial loyalty and to strive for the
attainment of a social order in Ireland based on Christian principles'*.
The sole dissenting voice was the Cabinet secretary, Maurice
Moynihan, who was thereafter excluded from Cabinet meetings. Sean
MacBride was to the fore in this decision. The advent of the Holy
Year in 1950 saw President Sean T. O'Kelly Taoiseach John A
Costello and the Minister of External Affairs Sean MacBride, all visit
Rome for the celebrations, with MacBride photographed holding the
key for the opening of the Holy Door. The importance of Catholicism
as the defining icon of Irish nationality was clear.

The repatriation of WB Yeats raised again the hopes of the Joyce
family that James' remains too might be repatriated to Ireland. He had
been buried in a temporary grave in Zurich in 1941.

James Joyce himself had been happy to use the good offices of the
Irish
diplomats in France and Switzerland, when he was trying to get
permission for his daughter Lucia, who was in a sanitarium, to leave
France after the German invasion. As usual with Joyce he interacted
with them on his own terms. Sean Murphy a Ministry official at
Vichy, wrote to Francis T. Cremins Charge at Berne on 13 January

1941 outlining these contacts with Joyce concerning his daughter. He wrote in a rather exasperated tone:

In July last Mr. James Joyce called to see me here in connection with his daughter whom he was anxious to have removed to Switzerland. As she holds a British passport I informed Mr. Joyce that I could not officially intervene on her behalf, having no 'locus standi' in the matter. I undertook, however, during a visit which I proposed to make to Paris in August to raise the matter unofficially, if a suitable occasion presented itself and in particular to endeavour to ascertain whether there would be any objection to Miss Joyce's leaving France in view of the fact that she was seriously ill. She suffers from a mental disease known as 'Hyperthuria' which apparently sometimes reduces her to a serious and dangerous condition. I did in fact visit Paris in August and found an opportunity of mentioning the case to a member of the German Embassy. He gave it as his personal opinion that no difficulty would be put in the way of Miss Joyce's journey on the part of the occupying authority...On my return to Vichy I informed Mr. Joyce that there would be no obstacle put in the way of his daughter's going to Switzerland. In November, however, I received a note from the German authorities to the effect that a journey to Switzerland by Miss Joyce who holds a British passport could not take place. I communicated this message to Mr. Joyce... He then enquired whether it would be well to have his daughter obtain an Irish passport. I told him she was perfectly entitled to claim citizenship by registration and that, if she should apply for registration, I would be prepared to issue her a passport valid for one year pending the decision of the Minister for Justice on her application... He, however, showed no inclination to follow it up at the time. I may add that he has never suggested applying for an Irish passport for himself and that his son also holds a British passport although at one time, when it looked as if he might be refused a French exit visa for that reason (being of military age), he did enquire about the procedure for getting an Irish one. He did not, however, pursue the matter, presumably because he was able to get a visa on his British passport[158].

- [158] . No. 394 DFA Paris Embassy 49/16

The Irish diplomatic service had also assisted Joyce financially, as the English solicitors Monroe & Company had prevailed upon the Irish High Commissioner in London to transmit to the Irish Minister at Vichy, for James Joyce (still a British subject), a small monthly remittance of £30, sanctioned by the Bank of England[159].

When the Secretary at External Affairs, Joseph Walshe a hyper-Catholic[160], heard of Joyce's sudden death, he instructed the *Charge* at Berne to, *"Please wire details about Joyce's death. If possible find out if he died a Catholic?*

Express sympathy with Mrs. Joyce and explain inability to attend funeral".

Cremins replied to Walsh on 17 January 1941.

Sudden attack of stomach trouble Thursday night, Doctor advised to go to hospital. On Friday morning Surgeon agreed and operation performed but something had burst resulting in perforation of stomach poisoning system, best specialist called, blood transfusions given. Slight hope up to Sunday evening then burst again and death 2 a.m. Monday. Patient bright, conscious up to Sunday evening. Best advice available, everything possible done by friends, doctors. Mrs. Joyce, son well as possible, I had already sent letter of sympathy; sending now more formal letter and explaining inability to leave here. Only last week he telephoned coming to see me. I had been trying to do something to obtain permission for daughter to leave occupied France for Switzerland. I have no information so far on other matter[161].

---

[159] . Jane Lidderdale & Mary Nicholson, *Dear Miss Weaver* Faber 1970. P. 397.

[160] .Akenson Harman Donald, *Conor A Biography of Conor Cruise O'Brien*, McGill-Queen's University Press 1994. P. 115. While Ambassador to the Vatican in 1949 Joseph Walshe advised Sean MacBride that John Charles McQuaid, Archbishop of Dublin, must not be made a Cardinal as that honour belonged historically to Armagh. He also said such a role would cause *"endless difficulties"* as McQuaid *"made continuous difficulties on matters of precedence whenever the Nuncio had to be present at a ceremony in the Pro Cathedral".*[No 362 6/9/1949 DFA]Walshe had briefed Monsignor Montini on the matter. Walshe declared himself a friend of McQuaid's for over 35 years.

[161] . No. 1 NAI DFA 339/124 Dublin 16 January 1941.

As usual with the Joyce family, there was a shortage of money and friends had to pay for the funeral. The single grave, numbered 1449 could only accommodate one coffin. Gordon Bowker writes that this *'was meant to be temporary, until Nora Joyce could get him repatriated to Ireland, and she asked Harriet Weaver, Joyce's Patron and literary executor, to look into this. Weaver approached Count O'Kelly, the Irish charge d'affaires in Paris,[* O'Kelly operated an unofficial Irish chancery in Paris when the officials moved to Vichy] *but the hostility to Joyce among the Catholic clergy, scholars and politicians was so intense that the request was refused'* [162] .The Minister of External Affairs was Eamon deValera.

Sean MacBride had a close personal and familial relationship with WB Yeats, but he had reasons to be inimical to Joyce, who had dishonored both his mother and father at the time of their marriage separation. Joyce wrote in March 1905, "*I have read in the Figaro of the divorce of the Irish Joan of Arc from her husband, Pius the Tenth. I suppose they will alter the Catholic Regulations to suit the case; an Italian comment says Irish genius is not domestic. Poor little U.I. indignant chap*"[163].

James Joyce also had rejected Maud Gonne's kind offer of assistance when he first came to Paris, preferring to act as though she had shunned him. She wrote graciously to him:

> 7 Avenue d'Eylau
> Paris

My Dear Mr. Joyce,

> *I was very sorry not to see you when you called last evening. The polite lie about my being in bed was diplomacy on the part of my concierge as at such an early hour I never retire to rest. The truth is that my little cousin who is staying with me took ill with diphtheria last Sunday, and I have been and still am nursing her and consequently am in quartine on account of the danger of infection. I shall be in quarantine for the usual 10 days or so. I do not like to invite you to the house till after the doctor tells me there is no*

[162] . Bowker Gordon James Joyce: A Biography Weidenfeld & Nicholson
[163] . Jordan Anthony J. *James Joyce Unplugged*, Westport Books 2017 p. 56.

danger for anyone coming here. There would, of course, be no possible danger seeing me out of doors, and if I can be of any use to you, come up any day at about 2 o'clock and I will come out and see you in the Trocadero Gardens.
This is a cold and inhospitable welcome. I am very sorry for Mr. Russell and Mr. Yeats have both spoken and written to me so much about you that I have been looking forward to making your acquaintance. However as I hear you are thinking of staying in Paris for some time, it is only a pleasure deferred.

With kind regards,
Sincerely yours
      Maud Gonne[164].

Though Joyce's mother later urged him to respond to Maud's invitation, James writing from the Grand Hotel Corneille on 21 February 1903, told her *"I have not gone to see Miss Gonne; nor do I intend to"*[165].

Maud had later disliked intensely Joyce's *Portrait of the Artist*, writing a critque to Yeats and accusing him [correctly] of praising the book without having read it. She wrote: *To have lived in Dublin & seen nothing but its ugliness & squalor, to have associated with those eager intensely living people & to have been able to describe nothing but dull futility & boredom seems to denote a nature to whom the stars would look like bits of tinsel paper. "Tell me the truth- confesses – you have not read the book yourself?*[166]

---

[164]. Jordan Anthony J. *Arthur Griffith with James Joyce and WB Yeats Liberating Ireland* Westport 2013 p. 57-8.
[165]. Jordan Anthony J. *Arthur Griffith with James Joyce & WB Yeats, Liberating Ireland*, Westport books 2013, p. 58.
[166]. MacBride White Anna & Norman Jeffares, Gonne Yeats Letters 1992 p.368.This view of *Portrait* is re-echoed over sixty years later by Conor Cruise O'Brien in an article titled *'The Artist As Pompous Prig"* in the *Sunday Tribune*, 31 January 1983. O'Brien asks, "But surely I can't be the only reader of A Portrait who gets put off by all this relentless rapture about self: fed up hearing so often how 'sensitive' Stephen is, how 'sordid' his family and fellow students, and,how 'coldly', 'quietly', or 'werarily' he addresses these, and to how impressive an effect".

Norman Jeffares writes in the introduction to the *Gonne- Yeats Letter" Maud's reaction to the plays of Synge and O'Casey may well have been caused by the same attitude of mind that shaped her view of Joyce: she had a distate for the elment of vulgarity, the bawdy tone, and the portrayal of mean or contemptible characters, particulary by Irish writers"[167].* In a letter to Yeats on 16th March 1916, Maud writes caustically, *"Tell Joyce to write his next book about Redmond & his colleagues. He might do them justice"[168].*

After the body of WB Yeats was repatriated to Ireland in September 1948, Nora began to have discreet inquiries made as to whether her husband's body could not be brought by the Eire Government to Dublin. While his grave remained in Zurich she felt she must remain there, though the climate was bad for her. But she was prepared to leave if her proposal was accepted. Miss Weaver had thought there was not much hope – *Mr. Joyce had antagonized the Irish priests and other Irishmen.*

Among those who took the most direct soundings on the matter was John Jermain Slocum. He was a wealthy American diplomat, scholar and bibliophile.

[167] . MacBride Anna & A. Norman Jeffares, *The Gonne- Yeats Letters* Pimlico 1992. P. 45.
[168] . ibid. p. 369.

[169]Slocum(1914-1997)and his wife Eileen.

He had travelled to Europe in June 1948 *"in search of material by and about Joyce. In Zurich I saw his widow and son. Joyce is buried in a beautiful little cemetery high on the Zuricherberg, but Mrs. Joyce will never be happy until his body is brought back to Ireland. She is a devout Catholic and feels that his body should rest in the land of his fathers"*. Slocum had met Miss Weaver who told him that she intended to donate the manuscript of *Finnegans Wake* to the National Library of Ireland and agreed that he could so inform the Director of the Library. Slocum did not do this but informed a bibliophile and Joyce an enthusiast named Quentin Keynes[170].

Slocum had a meeting in Dublin with President Sean T. O'Kelly in June 1948 and on 25 November he wrote a long and very carefully crafted letter to O'Kelly, referring to the recent repatriation of Yeats and asking:

"Without discounting the differences between the two men - their different relationships with their country and their countrymen, the difference in their reputation and the love which they inspired - I wonder if it is unreasonable to think that James Joyce might be so honored someday, and that in so honoring him, his country would be honoring itself?

I realize that this proposal is presumptuous coming from a foreigner. I realize that it has probably been made a dozen times by people of widely different tastes and points of view. I do not think that I or anyone else could ask for a definitive answer, but if you were to express to me even a belief that such a return of his body to Ireland was possible, I think that I could start his friends in Zurich, in Paris, in London, in New York and even in Dublin, working on it wholeheartedly"[171].

Slocum astutely adverted to a possible difficulty as he wrote:

'There is a possible stumbling block in Joyce's relationship with the Church -- the Church which he ostensibly repudiated, which he loved

---

[169] . He gathered the Yale University collection of Joyceania. It includes manuscripts of *'Dubliners', 'Chamber Music'* and *'Exiles'* and letters by and about Joyce. Together with Herbert Cahoon he compiled *'A Bibliography of James Joyce'*.

[170] . Jane Lidderdale & Mary Nicholson *Dear Miss Weaver* Faber 1970. P. 421.

[171] . Constantine Curran Papers Special Collections UCD.

to his dying day and which was the fount of his inspiration. Through his Jesuit education the Church was the mould in which his genius was formed".

Slocum referred to the stand taken by *Osservatore Romano* concerning Joyce's work in an article Oct 2 1937, saying that *"there is sufficient evidence that the Church itself recognizes his contribution to the tradition of Catholic letters. In an article on Irish literature on that day he was described objectively and dispassionately in terms of his contribution to European letters.*
I have digressed long enough concerning ths matter. I would appreciate an expression of opinion by you concerning it, official or otherwise. Meanwhile thank you again for an enjoyable visit with you in Dublin[172].
The actual reference to Joyce reads " *And finally James Joyce, of European fame, inconoclast and rebel, who after having sought to renovate the old naturalism, attempted in Ulysses, to translate plastically the inner reality, and, who, in Work in Progress, in an experiment, both oneric and linguistic, is seeking to open up new paths for the expression of human sentient".* October 22 1937.

Slocum's letter to President Sean T. O'Kelly was officially directed through the Office of An Taoiseach, John A Costello and to Sean MacBride, Minister of External Affairs in the new Coalition Government. Of course O'Kelly and MacBride had a long-standing relationship, with each having confidence in the other[173]. MacBride directed the letter to his personal private secretary, the poet-diplomat Valentine Ironmonger. The latter had taken a new official to the Department, Conor Cruise O'Brien, under his wing as second secretary in the protocol and miscellaneous section. MacBride has written, *"My private secretary was Val Ironmonger, who got on very well with Conor Cruise O'Brien. Val was a writer, a poet and had a certain amount of sympathy with Cruise O'Brien. Val Ironmonger*

[172] . At the time of publication in 1937 Gerald Griffin wrote to Paul Leon commenting on the tribute to *Ulysses* and *Work in Progress* in the Vatican newspaper writing *"The Dublin puritans will be shocked that the official organ of the Vatican praised Joyce".* The James Joyce Paul Leon Papers The National Library of Ireland p. 100. 1992. Compiled by Catherine Foley.

[173] . Sean MacBride *That Day's Struggle pp. 128-9.*

was capable, nice and very pleasant to work with. I must have been an extremely difficult boss for him". MacBride wrote of Cruise O'Brien, "I felt I couldn't trust him. He wrote articles attacking me under false names in the Leader and other newspapers"[174]. Cruise O'Brien later wrote of MacBride, 'It is true that Mr. MacBride's scowl-like features, old-fashioned aristocratic airs, and cinematic foreign accent appear less ominous and more human to anyone who has enjoyed with him an excellent diner at (say) Ramponneau's in the Avenue Marceau.However, this subject is one on which I do really suffer from over –information, so I must not pass on that dread contagion'[175]. Joseph Walshe, no friend of James Joyce, was then Irish Ambassador at the Vatican. Ironmonger, whom one might expect might have some admiration for the writer James Joyce, spent several months challenging the contents of Slocum's reading of the article in L'Osservatore Romano, ostensibly lauding Joyce. He got a diplomat at the Irish Embassy to Italy, HR MacDonald, to locate the article, translate it and interview the author, a Catholic priest. He then reported "In view of the stand taken by Osservatore Romano concerning his work, there is not sufficient evidence that the Church itself recognizes his contribution to the tradition of Catholic Letters". James Joyce has not been examined officially as a result of the priest's article. Ironmonger wrote to Paddy Lynch, Costello's economic advisor at the Department that the Article could hardly be construed as "evidence that the Church itself recognizes Joyce's contribution to the tradition of Catholic letters". Ironmonger was bringing in the verdict he knew Sean MacBride and the Government required.

Sean was very close to the Catholic Church authorities on an official level. His first action after becoming Minister of External Affairs in 1948 was to draft a message to Pope Pius XII on behalf of the Government offering "my colleagues and myself desire to repose at the feet of Your Holiness". He wrote to Cardinal D'Alton, "I should be indebted to Your Grace if Your Grace would say a prayer asking

---

[174]. MacBride Sean *That Day's Struggle* p. 181-2. For text of that article cf. *Sean MacBride*, Anthony J. Jordan, Blackwater Press 1993, pp. 138-9

[175]. Anthology- Vol 11 *A Biography of Conor Cruise O'Brien 'Now They Talk of Over-Information'* Donald Harman Akenson 1994.

God to give me the wisdom necessary to carry out my new duties well and faithfully".

John Slocum wrote to Constantine Curran, a lifelong friend and associate of Joyce, on 11 March 1949:

"I had a very nice letter the other day from Georgio Joyce...I wrote a long and impassioned letter to Sean T. O'Kelly several months ago proving conclusively that Joyce was a good Catholic and that his body should be brought home to Ireland because his widow would have it that way and because he was a large stone in the tower of Irish literature, or rather world literature. I have had no answer...If you should see him tell him to get after his secretary. I am waiting for an answer[176].

Slocum never got a reply to his letter. It was copied to the Taoiseach's Department on 13 July and thence to External Affairs. The immediate response to the Taoiseach's Department read, *Please ask the Aras what action, if any, they have taken on Mr. Slocum's letter. Have they acknowledged it?* It transpired that the original letter '*could not be traced*' at an Aras and they couldn't say whether any answer issued in November 1948 A note on the Department of An Taoiseach of 15 July 1949 read "*Spoke to Taoiseach. No Action*".

David Norris, a famous Dublin Joycean, was friendly with Maria Jolas, a member of Joyce's Parisian circle. She informed him that the matter of Joyce's repatriation went to the Government, but for some reason Sean MacBride '*refused to support it'* and the matter was left[177]. Senator Norris informed me that Nora Joyce passed on this information to Jolas.

Paul Leon, Joyce's longtime friend and admirer, rescued material from Joyce's wartime flat in Paris. He deposited pictures and some papers with Joyce's lawyer. He deposited others with the Irish Ambassador, under a 50 year seal, with instructions for their transfer to the National Library of Ireland, should he not survive the war.

---

[176]. ibid

[177]. Norris David Senator *Sean MacBride The Assassin's Cloak* in Speaking Ill of the Dead, Myles Dungan (ED) New Ireland 2007.

Leon was arrested by the Nazis and died in Auschwitz in April 1942[178].

The material was exhibited in Paris at Librairie La Hune in 1949 and in London at the Institute for Contemporary Arts in 1950. Sean MacBride was invited to perform the opening or become its Patron in Paris. His official refusal was signed by Ironmonger. It said; *Mr. MacBride Minister External Affairs has asked me to refer to your letter and to say he regrets very much he will not be able to open the James Joyce Exhibition on 25 October*. However Mr. Ashley Clarke, British Ambassador in Paris lent his name as Patron to the Memorial Exhibition.

On the invitation for the London exhibition, Conor Cruise O'Brien wrote; *"Before his departure to the Continent the Minister of External Affairs Mr. Sean MacBride, asked me to inform you that he regrets he was not able to be in London for the Private Viewing and opening of the James Joyce Exhibition, which was attended by Mr. John Dulanty High Commissioner for Ireland. The Minister would like very much to visit the Exhibition if he should be in London while it is still on"*[179].

Harriet Weaver, who had long been one of Joyce's Patrons, became his literary executor. Joyce had been sending her completed pages of *Finnegans Wake* over many years. She was then in possession of the complete manuscript and began to consider the best home for it. She contacted T.S Eliot who asked had she considered Dublin. She wrote *"I did think of one of the Dublin libraries for Mr. Joyce's manuscripts. It was to the British Museum I inclined as more accessible – greater number of writers and students. It would be helpful if you consulted some of your Irish friends privately and tentatively without mentioning my name"*. Sometime later, Miss Weaver met Eliot and said that she was almost decided on Ireland, adding that Mr. Constantine Curran would be able to advise her on this. Writing to Miss Weaver, Curran dismissed the claims of the other Dublin libraries before adding, *there remains the National*

---

[178] . Jane Lidderdale & Mary Nicholson p. 397.
[179] . Department Foreign Affairs 16 June 1950 239/116.

Library and I have no hesitation in recommending it alone. It is a modern and admirably managed library of first rate standing, with the same privileges as the British Museum and of the Advocates Library. It has a valuable and growing Manuscript Department particularly in regard to modern literature in Ireland i.e. from the 18th century...I am entirely of T.S. Eliot's opinion that every serious student of Joyce is inseparable from Dublin...There is further Joyce's personal association with the National Library of Ireland. I know his seat in it and can't go near the place without thinking of him. This Library makes a chapter of Ulysses. Anyway the National Library of Ireland is, to my mind, the natural destination of the Manuscript if you remain with your present intention and so far as I can honestly and freely interpret the mind of our dear friend, it would be his desire[180].

Harriet needed little persuasion. Mr. Joyce should return there and she had confidence in Mr. Curran's advice. Her intention was to bequest the Manuscript to the National Library of Ireland

Nora Joyce contacted Miss Weaver to say that she had been
"extremely upset"
to read in a cutting from the *Irish Independent* sent to her from Galway that her husband's letters to Paul Leon and *"documents relating to the affairs of the Joyce family during the period 1934-1940"* had been given to the National Library of Ireland. She considered that the wishes of the family should have been consulted and that as Ireland had *"never appreciated"* her husband, the Library would not have been her choice. Harriet was asked *"to take the matter in hand"* but responded that it was impossible for her to do anything. But she decided that she must set out in detail the steps leading up to her decision to bequeath the manuscript of *Finnegan's Wake* to Ireland. She wrote:
"In favor of Dublin I was also influenced by the fact that of the entire obituary notices of Mr. Joyce that I had seen at that time, the Dublin notices were the best. The Times had a very poor article and the Times Literary Supplement a disgracefully obtuse article.

---

[180] . Lidderdale Jane & Mary Nicholson *Dear Miss Weaver* Faber 1970 p. 380 passim.

Considering all these things I decided to bequeath the manuscript to the National Library of Ireland and I made a codicil to my Will to that effect. But if Mrs. Joyce strongly disapproves I could alter it. I should not like to leave the manuscript to any institution in America, which country has to my mind, become unbearably aggressive since President Roosevelts' lamentable death[181].

Miss Evelyn Cotton, a member of the English Players in Zurich, reported to Miss Weaver that Mrs. Joyce had become reconciled to the National Library of Ireland getting the manuscript. But a few months later Nora Joyce shocked Miss Weaver by her "*bombshell*" renewed opposition to her plan, due to her annoyance with the recent negative reaction to her husband from Ireland. Nora was "*without a good word to say for the Irish*". Patricia Hutchins [writer and author of *James Joyce's Dublin* married to Robert Grecan] was informed by Miss Weaver of Nora's attitude. Hutchins then with Miss Weaver's permission, contacted the Irish High Commissioner in London, John Dulanty, saying that if the Irish Government wanted the Manuscript of *Finnegans Wake*, they should take some action. Sean MacBride was apprised of this. He wrote brazenly to Nora Joyce on 12 July 1950:

"*I understand from some close friends of yours that the question of the disposition of the Manuscript of Finnegan's Wake may be arising in the near future. A suggestion has been made that it might go to the National Library of Ireland...I should like you to know that I personally and I am sure my colleagues in the Irish Government, as well as the Library itself, are deeply sensitive of how desirable it is from the nation's point of view that the manuscript of this great work should be deposited in your husband's native city. We are proud that James Joyce, one of the greatest Europeans of his time was also a son of Ireland and we feel that the presence in the Library of the manuscript of which may be his greatest work would be a fitting commemoration of that fact*"[182].

---

[181]. *Dear Miss Weaver* . p. 411.
[182]. Department Foreing Affairs 5 339/174.

Nora did not reply to the Minister but sent his letter to Miss Weaver, without a covering note. Miss Weaver got Maria Jolas, a longtime Joycean friend, to go to Zurich to mediate with Nora. She reported to Miss Weaver that the Irish *"must be indeed very dull-witted if the irony of it all escapes them"*. Some months later Miss Weaver sought to contact Nora hoping that she would be reconciled with Dublin. However Nora was very ill and Georgio told her that both he and his mother were *"still utterly hostile to Dublin"*. Miss Weaver thought this *'quite prejudicial"* but she then favored the British Museum. Nora died on 10 April 1951 and had to be buried apart from her husband. Later a new grave was opened where James, Nora, their son Georgio and his wife are buried in Fluntern Cemetery Zurich.

In June 1951 Patricia Hutchins escorted Miss Weaver to the British Museum to meet George D. Painter of the Department of Printed Books and on 27 June she handed over the manuscript to the British Museum.

Miss Weaver also had the manuscript of *A Portrait of the Artist as a Young Man,* the placing of which she had not discussed with Nora Joyce. She wrote to the Director of the National Library of Ireland, Dr. Hayes, offering him the manuscript. She presented it through the Irish Embassy in London. It was graciously accepted by the Ambassador FH Boland who remarked that he met Joyce frequently at the Irish Embassy in Paris during 1932-34. He added *"Joyce was always prepared to listen to Dubliners born and bred like myself"*. Miss Weaver also presented the *wonderful illuminated initial letters Lucia made (urged on by her father) for the Chaucer A.B.C.* adding, *"I think Lucia would be pleased too"*.

PRESIDENT HIGGINS VISIT IN 2018

In June 2018 President Michael D. Higgins, on a state visit to
Switzerland, visited the Joyce family grave at Fluntern cemetery in
Zurich and laid white roses on the grave over-looking the city. Beside
a seated statue of Joyce, Mr. Higgins thanked the city of Zurich for
maintaining the grave *"today and all the days since the 1940s"*. In
doing so he made some official reparation for the way his country had
rejected the family's wish to be repatriated back to lIreland.

Chapter 21.

Sean MacBride in Merrion Square in 1983 to witness unveiling of sculpture in honour Nelson Mandela,

After leaving party politics Sean MacBride went on to become an international statesman receiving high honors as a winner of the Nobel Peace Prize, the Lenin Medal and the American Medal of Honour. He became a full-time Secretary General to the Geneva based International Commission of Jurists, meaning that he had to live in Geneva.

Sean was a charming man to those he liked, and if he liked you, you could do no wrong. He loved the good life and would go out to dinner every second evening, funds permitting. But he was never active socially without a purpose. He had no small talk at all, relying on serious topics at all times. He loved the company of women and like his father was attractive to women. He was rarely disappointed by those he sought out for his special attention. He found that women were better to work with. He found them more efficient than men, being less independent, and more willing to follow instructions. He liked to hire Irish women when working abroad[183].

Sean remained true to his mother all his life and rarely spoke of his father. The fact that his mother and father parted in such bitter circumstances was a lifelong sorrow for him. In later years he had begun to speak very distantly of his father and mother together. At the opening of the Michael Davitt Memorial Museum in Straide Co. Mayo in 1984 Sean gave the oration and said speaking of Davitt:

The fact that he was a Mayoman and that my father came from Mayo probably also contributed to my interest in and admiration for Michael Davitt.... The principles of the French Revolution reached America largely through the United Irishmen and Tone. Later Michael Davitt, John O'Leary, Roger Casement and my own parents were all closely involved in the development of the movement which led to the demolition of colonialism in the world. Indeed in an odd way, because of the close links between the Irish revolutionaries and the Boers and the Indians ... Ireland was blamed for sowing the seeds of anti-imperialism and anti-colonialism in Africa and India[184]

Maud had never been afraid of death. She passed that on to her son, as she had got it from her father. As she reached her eighties, she sometimes longed for death. Most of her contemporaries were dead. One of the people who became a very good friend to her in later life was Michaeal MacLiammoir. She once told him that old age was hell. She remained right to the end a fanatical hater of England. Francis MacManus, a Radio Eireann producer got her to do a series of broadcast talks on her long life. He wrote of her, "*Her age had its beauty. Her hair, fine as silk and still glossy, was whorled over her ears in an antique way...There was witchcraft in her voice...When she finished...she smoked a cigarette and talked in quieter tones*"[185].

The poet Paul Durcan, a blood relation to the Gonnes and the MacBrides, through his Grandmother Eileen Wilson and his Uncle

---

[183] . Jordan Anthony, *Sean MacBride A biography* p. 161-2. Tiernan MacBride, Sean's son, launched my biography of his father in 1993.

[184] .Sean MacBride, A Biography, Anthony J. Jordan Blackwater Press 1993 p. 186.

[185] . The Capuchin Annual 1960.

Joseph MacBride, was taken by his mother to see Maud Gonne in her mid-eighties. Sean and Kid announced the visitors to Maud, whom the poet saw *"In the rubble of her beautiful face"* and whose mother, Eileen Wilson's daughter, saw *"a disloyal wife"* who betrayed *"that gay man"*[186].

Finally on 27 April 1953 aged 86 years, she received the Last Sacraments of the Catholic Church. She asked Iseult to get her baby George's booties from her handbag where she had always carried them and told her to make sure they stayed with her. Then she died peacefully. She was buried in Glasnevin Cemetery amid many of her former colleagues and friends.

An anonymous article in the *Irish Times* was mildly critical of Maud saying *"she could or would talk about nothing except the manifold sins and wickedness of the British in Ireland...There was a touch of magic about her, which persisted into the sourness of old age"*. Sean's long suffering wife, Catalina Bulfin, wrote graciously to the newspaper:

"I have lived twenty six years with Madame, and sourness and frustration are two things I should never have remotely connected with her. Sourness is for people who have not achieved, or who lack appreciation for, their achievements and are small enough to mind, but in Madame's case there was plenty of appreciation from the people about whom she cared. All over the country there are people who bless her name. Frustration is for little people... Nothing ever stopped Madame once set on a course, as various Governments and people have found out from time to time".

MacBride family Grave in Glasnevin Cemetery.

---

[186] .Durcan Paul, The *MacBride Dynasty* in *The Laughter of Mothers, Harvill* Secker 2007. pp. 71-2.

SELECT BIBLIOGRAPHY

Andrews CS. *Dublin Made Me* Mercier 1979.

Balliet Conrad *The lives - and lies - of Maud Gonne* Eire – Ireland cxliv no. 3 (Fall 1979)

Cardozo Nancy *Maud Gonne* Victor Golancz 1979

Fallon Donal 16 Lives *John MacBride* 2015

Foster Roy *The Apprentice Mage* 1997

Gonne MacBride Maud *A Servant of the Queen* Gollancz 1938

Gonne Maud Irish Nationalist Writings 1895-1946 Steele Karen Ed. Dublin 2004

Samuel Levenson *Maud Gonne* Cassell 1973.

Jeffares A Norman & Anna MacBride White *The Gonne-Yeats Letters 1893-1938*

Jordan Anthony J. *Major John MacBride* Westport Historical Society 1991

> *Sean MacBride* Blackwater Press 1993
>
> *Conor Cruise O'Brien* Blackwater Press 1994
>
> *Boer War to Easter Rising Writings of John Mac Bride* 1996
>
> *Willie Yeats & The Gonne MacBrides* Westport 1997
>
> *The Yeats Gonne MacBride Triangle* Westport 2000.
>
> *WB Yeats Vain; Glorious; Lout* Westport 2013,
>
> *Arthur Griffith with James Joyce & WB Yeats – Liberating Ireland* Westport 2013.
>
> *James Joyce Unplugged* Westport 2017

Kelly John [ed) *Colected Letters of WB Yeats 1965-1895* Oxford 1985

McCardle Dorothy, *The Irish Republic* Gollancz 1937

MacDermott Eithne *Clann na Poblachta* Cork University Press 1998

Magny Anna Maud Gonne *Realite at Myth Analyse d'une presense historique et litteraire* [Rennes; University of Rennes 30 March 1992].

Mathews Ann, *Renegades Irish Republican* Women Cork 2010

Saddlemyer Ann *Becoming George* Oxford 2003

Neeson Eoin *The Civil War in Ireland* Mercier 1966

Shiubhlaigh Maire *The Splendid Years* Duffy 1955

Stuart Francis *Blacklist, Section H* Penguin 1982

Ward Margaret *Maud Gonne* Pandora 1990

Young Ella *Flowering Dusk; things remembered accurately and in accurately* New York 1945

Index